# HTML 4
FOR
# DUMMIES®
## QUICK REFERENCE
### 2ND EDITION

## by Deborah S. Ray
## and Eric J. Ray

IDG Books Worldwide, Inc.
An International Data Group Company

Foster City, CA ✦ Chicago, IL ✦ Indianapolis, IN ✦ New York, NY

**HTML 4 For Dummies® Quick Reference, 2nd Edition**

Published by
**IDG Books Worldwide, Inc.**
An International Data Group Company
919 E. Hillsdale Blvd.
Suite 400
Foster City, CA 94404
www.idgbooks.com (IDG Books Worldwide Web site)
www.dummies.com (Dummies Press Web site)

Library of Congress Control Number: 00-103391

ISBN: 0-7645-0721-4

Printed in the United States of America

10 9 8 7 6 5 4 3 2 1

2P/QU/QY/QQ/IN

Distributed in the United States by IDG Books Worldwide, Inc.

Distributed by CDG Books Canada Inc. for Canada; by Transworld Publishers Limited in the United Kingdom; by IDG Norge Books for Norway; by IDG Sweden Books for Sweden; by IDG Books Australia Publishing Corporation Pty. Ltd. for Australia and New Zealand; by TransQuest Publishers Pte Ltd. for Singapore, Malaysia, Thailand, Indonesia, and Hong Kong; by Gotop Information Inc. for Taiwan; by ICG Muse, Inc. for Japan; by Intersoft for South Africa; by Eyrolles for France; by International Thomson Publishing for Germany, Austria and Switzerland; by Distribuidora Cuspide for Argentina; by LR International for Brazil; by Galileo Libros for Chile; by Ediciones ZETA S.C.R. Ltda. for Peru; by WS Computer Publishing Corporation, Inc., for the Philippines; by Contemporanea de Ediciones for Venezuela; by Express Computer Distributors for the Caribbean and West Indies; by Micronesia Media Distributor, Inc. for Micronesia; by Chips Computadoras S.A. de C.V. for Mexico; by Editorial Norma de Panama S.A. for Panama; by American Bookshops for Finland.

For general information on IDG Books Worldwide's books in the U.S., please call our Consumer Customer Service department at 800-762-2974. For reseller information, including discounts and premium sales, please call our Reseller Customer Service department at 800-434-3422.

For information on where to purchase IDG Books Worldwide's books outside the U.S., please contact our International Sales department at 317-596-5530 or fax 317-572-4002.

For consumer information on foreign language translations, please contact our Customer Service department at 1-800-434-3422, fax 317-572-4002, or e-mail rights@idgbooks.com.

For information on licensing foreign or domestic rights, please phone +1-650-653-7098.

For sales inquiries and special prices for bulk quantities, please contact our Order Services department at 800-434-3422 or write to the address above.

For information on using IDG Books Worldwide's books in the classroom or for ordering examination copies, please contact our Educational Sales department at 800-434-2086 or fax 317-572-4005.

For press review copies, author interviews, or other publicity information, please contact our Public Relations department at 650-653-7000 or fax 650-653-7500.

For authorization to photocopy items for corporate, personal, or educational use, please contact Copyright Clearance Center, 222 Rosewood Drive, Danvers, MA 01923, or fax 978-750-4470.

# About the Authors

Just a word about us — so that you know who the "we" is that we refer to throughout this book.

We are Deborah and Eric Ray, owners of RayComm, Inc., a technical communication consulting company. For the most part, we write computer books, including *Dummies 101: HTML* and *Netscape Composer For Dummies,* to name a couple. In fact (if you can pardon a little bragging), *HTML For Dummies Quick Reference* (this book's 1st edition) and *Dummies 101: HTML* won international awards at the 1997 Society for Technical Communication Technical Publications Competition. And, when we're not trapped under mounds of book drafts, we also give occasional seminars on HTML and Internet-related topics, and we take on other techno-jargon-ese-into-English translation projects.

I, Deborah Ray (my friends call me Deb), have been a technical communicator for the past seven years and, among other projects, work on developing *The Official TECHWR-L* Web site — the Web site supporting the technical communication community. I taught technical writing to students at Utah State University and Oklahoma State University. I also have a variety of technical experiences, including creating various computer and engineering documents for sundry purposes. My areas of emphasis include writing, designing, and illustrating documents to meet various audiences' information needs.

I, Eric Ray (my friends call me, well, Eric), have been involved with the Internet for eight years and have made numerous presentations and written several papers about HTML and online information. (I like to hear myself write.) My technical experience includes creating and maintaining the TECHWR-L listserv list (the oldest and largest discussion forum for technical communicators) as well as implementing and running Internet servers. I guess you'd say that I'm a Webmaster. As a technical communicator, I focus on making "techie" information easy for normal people to understand.

Thanks to our combined skills, we've reached stereotypical geek status, having side-by-side home computer workstations at which we work hours and hours every day. Our cats perch on the monitors, stare at us, and attempt to supervise our work. (Actually, we think they're just keeping their tummies warm.)

# ABOUT IDG BOOKS WORLDWIDE

Welcome to the world of IDG Books Worldwide.

IDG Books Worldwide, Inc., is a subsidiary of International Data Group, the world's largest publisher of computer-related information and the leading global provider of information services on information technology. IDG was founded more than 30 years ago by Patrick J. McGovern and now employs more than 9,000 people worldwide. IDG publishes more than 290 computer publications in over 75 countries. More than 90 million people read one or more IDG publications each month.

Launched in 1990, IDG Books Worldwide is today the #1 publisher of best-selling computer books in the United States. We are proud to have received eight awards from the Computer Press Association in recognition of editorial excellence and three from Computer Currents' First Annual Readers' Choice Awards. Our best-selling ...For Dummies® series has more than 50 million copies in print with translations in 31 languages. IDG Books Worldwide, through a joint venture with IDG's Hi-Tech Beijing, became the first U.S. publisher to publish a computer book in the People's Republic of China. In record time, IDG Books Worldwide has become the first choice for millions of readers around the world who want to learn how to better manage their businesses.

Our mission is simple: Every one of our books is designed to bring extra value and skill-building instructions to the reader. Our books are written by experts who understand and care about our readers. The knowledge base of our editorial staff comes from years of experience in publishing, education, and journalism — experience we use to produce books to carry us into the new millennium. In short, we care about books, so we attract the best people. We devote special attention to details such as audience, interior design, use of icons, and illustrations. And because we use an efficient process of authoring, editing, and desktop publishing our books electronically, we can spend more time ensuring superior content and less time on the technicalities of making books.

You can count on our commitment to deliver high-quality books at competitive prices on topics you want to read about. At IDG Books Worldwide, we continue in the IDG tradition of delivering quality for more than 30 years. You'll find no better book on a subject than one from IDG Books Worldwide.

John Kilcullen
Chairman and CEO
IDG Books Worldwide, Inc.

*Eighth Annual Computer Press Awards ≥1992*

*Ninth Annual Computer Press Awards ≥1993*

*Tenth Annual Computer Press Awards ≥1994*

*Eleventh Annual Computer Press Awards ≥1995*

# Dedication

To each other . . . and Ashleigh and Alex, who have helped us learn what's important in life.

# Authors' Acknowledgments

We owe many people a big round of thanks for helping us complete this book. We are most grateful to Gareth Hancock, Jill Pisoni, and Steve Hayes at IDG Books Worldwide, Inc., for their confidence in us to write and maintain these HTML books. Thanks to Melba Hopper for the help and guidance on previous editions of this book. A special thanks to Rev Mengle for his guidance and contributions to the second "incarnation of this book," and to Susan Christophersen for her guidance on this edition.

We also want to thank the whole crew of people at IDG Books who helped produce this book. A big thank you goes to our copy editor, also Susan Christophersen, and to our technical editor, Greg Guntle. We also send our appreciation to the book's indexer, York Production Services, the production coordinator, Maridee Ennis, and the entire production team. Each of these highly competent people contributed a great deal to this book — and to our sanity.

Also, a great big ol' thanks to Megg Bonar, former acquisitions editor at IDG Books, for the "foot-in-the-door" and the kind notes left in her desk . . . .

# Publisher's Acknowledgments

We're proud of this book; please register your comments through our IDG Books Worldwide Online Registration Form located at http://my2cents.dummies.com.

Some of the people who helped bring this book to market include the following:

## Acquisitions, Editorial, and Media Development

**Project Editor:** Susan Christophersen

*Previous Edition: Melba Hopper*

**Acquisitions Editor:** Steve Hayes

**Copy Editor:** Susan Christophersen

**Technical Editor:** Greg Guntle

**Editorial Manager:** Rev Mengle

## Production

**Project Coordinator:** Maridee Ennis

**Layout and Graphics:** Amy Adrian, Tracy K. Oliver

**Proofreaders:** Laura Albert, Corey Bowen, John Greenough, Marianne Santy, York Production Services, Inc.

**Indexer:** York Production Services, Inc.

## General and Administrative

**IDG Books Worldwide, Inc.:** John Kilcullen, CEO

**IDG Books Technology Publishing Group:** Richard Swadley, Senior Vice President and Publisher; Walter R. Bruce III, Vice President and Publisher; Joseph Wikert, Vice President and Publisher; Mary Bednarek, Vice President and Director, Product Development; Andy Cummings, Publishing Director, General User Group; Mary C. Corder, Editorial Director; Barry Pruett, Publishing Director

**IDG Books Consumer Publishing Group:** Roland Elgey, Senior Vice President and Publisher; Kathleen A. Welton, Vice President and Publisher; Kevin Thornton, Acquisitions Manager; Kristin A. Cocks, Editorial Director

**IDG Books Internet Publishing Group:** Brenda McLaughlin, Senior Vice President and Publisher; Sofia Marchant, Online Marketing Manager

**IDG Books Production for Branded Press:** Debbie Stailey, Director of Production; Cindy L. Phipps, Manager of Project Coordination, Production Proofreading, and Indexing; Tony Augsburger, Manager of Prepress, Reprints, and Systems; Laura Carpenter, Production Control Manager; Shelley Lea, Supervisor of Graphics and Design; Debbie J. Gates, Production Systems Specialist; Robert Springer, Supervisor of Proofreading; Kathie Schutte, Production Supervisor

**Packaging and Book Design:** Patty Page, Manager, Promotions Marketing

◆

The publisher would like to give special thanks to Patrick J. McGovern, without whom this book would not have been possible.

◆

# Contents at a Glance

HTML 4: The Big Picture ............................................1

Part I: Creating an HTML Page ...............................17

Part II: Spinning Your HTML Web .............................35

Part III: Using Images in Your Web Pages ...............47

Part IV: Using Images for Linking ...........................67

Part V: Making Effective Web Pages ........................87

Part VI: Setting Background and Text Characteristics ........99

Part VII: Serving HTML to the World ....................115

Part VIII: Developing Forms ................................123

Part IX: Framing Your Site .................................145

Part X: Developing Style Sheets ..........................157

Appendix A: HTML Tags ....................................175

Appendix B: Special Symbols ..............................203

Appendix C: Cascading Style Sheet Reference .................209

Index ...............................................................217

# Table of Contents

**HTML 4: The Big Picture** ...................................... 1

**Part I: Creating an HTML Page** ...................... 17

About Text and Tags ................................................... 18
Formatting text ................................................ 19
Nesting tags ................................................ 19
Including HTML Structure Tags ........................................ 20
The !DOCTYPE tag ................................................ 21
The <HTML> tag ................................................ 22
The <HEAD> and <TITLE> tags ........................ 22
The <META> tag ................................................ 23
The <BODY> tag ................................................ 23
Using Basic HTML Tags ................................................ 24
Making headings ................................................ 25
Making paragraphs ................................................ 27
Emphasizing text ................................................ 28
Making lists ................................................ 30
Setting off text ................................................ 33

**Part II: Spinning Your HTML Web** ................. 35

About Links ................................................ 36
About URLs ................................................ 36
Anatomy of URLs ................................................ 37
Absolute and relative URLs ................................................ 38
About Anchors ................................................ 40
Making Your First Links ................................................ 41
Linking to documents within your site ........................ 41
Linking to pages out on the Web ........................ 42
Linking to other stuff on the Internet ........................ 44
Making Links within Documents ................................................ 44
Making internal links ................................................ 44
Marking internal targets ................................................ 45

**Part III: Using Images in Your Web Pages** ....47

Adding Images ................................................ 48
Creating images for HTML documents ........................ 51
Choosing colors carefully ................................................ 52
Borrowing images ................................................ 54
Creating transparent images ................................................ 55
Addressing Image Download Speed ................................................ 57
Reducing file size ................................................ 58
Specifying image size ................................................ 59

Controlling Image Alignment ...............................................60
    Changing alignment ................................................61
    Using multiple alignment options ..........................63
    Using alignment to create interesting effects ..........64
    Using horizontal and vertical spacing ....................65

## Part IV: Using Images for Linking .................67

Making Images into Links ............................................68
    Using thumbnails ...................................................70
Creating Clickable Images ...........................................74
    Adding the image ...................................................75
    Mapping clickable areas .........................................76
    Mapping a rectangle ...............................................78
    Mapping a circle ....................................................79
    Mapping a polygon .................................................80
    Defining the map ....................................................81

## Part V: Making Effective Web Pages ............87

Developing Tables .......................................................88
Embedding Horizontal Rules .........................................91
Forcing Line Breaks ....................................................93
Providing Author and Contact Information ....................94
    Using an address tag ..............................................95
    Using an e-mail link ...............................................96

## Part VI: Setting Background
## and Text Characteristics ..............................99

Applying a Color Background .......................................100
    Finding RGB values ...............................................102
Applying an Image Background .....................................102
    Finding images to use ...........................................104
Setting Document Text Colors .....................................105
    Changing text colors .............................................106
    Changing link colors .............................................107
Specifying Text Alignment ..........................................108
Using Type Specifications ...........................................110

## Part VII: Serving HTML to the World ..........115

About Servers ...........................................................116
Determining Your URL ................................................116
Getting Documents onto the Server .............................117
Getting Server Programs ............................................118
Linking Things Automatically .....................................119
Including a Counter ...................................................120

## *Part VIII: Developing Forms* ......................*123*

Creating a Basic Form ....................................................................124
Including Form Components ...........................................................126
    Including Submit and Reset buttons .......................................127
    Including check boxes, radio buttons, and more .................128
    Making check boxes ................................................................129
    Making radio buttons ..............................................................132
    Using other input types .........................................................134
    Including select lists ..............................................................136
    Including text areas ................................................................139
    Including fieldsets and legends .............................................141

## *Part IX: Framing Your Site* .........................*145*

About Frames ..................................................................................146
Developing Content ........................................................................148
Developing Alternative Content ....................................................149
Establishing the Frameset Document ...........................................149
Setting Up the Frames ...................................................................152
Setting Up Links and Targets ........................................................154
Testing Your Framed Site ...............................................................155

## *Part X: Developing Style Sheets* ...................*157*

About Style Sheets .........................................................................158
Connecting Style Sheets to HTML Documents ............................160
    Embedding style sheets .........................................................161
    Linking style sheets ................................................................162
    Creating the style sheet file ..................................................163
    Putting in the link ..................................................................163
Developing Style Sheets .................................................................164
    Constructing style rules ........................................................165
    Applying style rules ...............................................................166
    Setting a font for an entire document ..................................168
    Specifying text and background colors ................................170
    Specifying background images ..............................................171
    Specifying image alignment ..................................................172
Gathering a Few Final Tips ............................................................173

## *Appendix A: HTML Tags* .........................*175*

## *Appendix B: Special Symbols* ...................*203*

## Appendix C: Cascading Style Sheet Reference ...................209

Cascading Style Sheets Reference ...........................................210
Font properties ...........................................................................211
Text properties ...........................................................................212
Box properties .............................................................................213
Color and background properties ...........................................215
Classification properties ...........................................................216

## Index ................................................................217

# HTML: The Big Picture

The Big Picture covers the *whats, wheres, whys,* and some *hows* of HTML — a great place to get started if you're a complete novice with this stuff. And even if you already have some clue as to what HTML is all about, this part can help you understand how the whole HTML/Internet/intranet/World Wide Web/WWW/Web business fits together.

## In this part. . .

- ✔ What You See
- ✔ Tools Table
- ✔ The Basics
- ✔ What You Can Do

# What You See — HTML Documents in the Editor

When developing HTML documents in an HTML editor, you'll see a bunch of code that may, at a glance, look like gobbledygook. With a closer look, though, you'll see that the HTML document contains fairly intuitive tags and attributes.

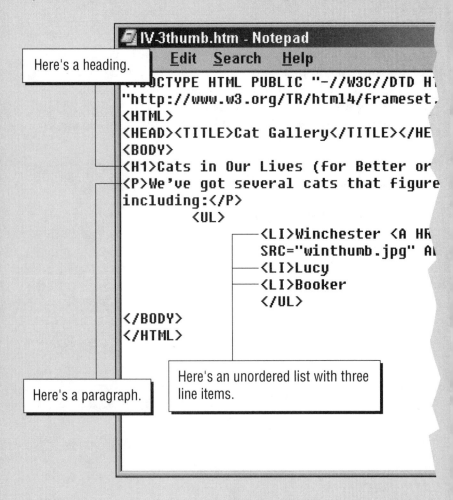

Here's a heading.

Here's a paragraph.

Here's an unordered list with three line items.

2

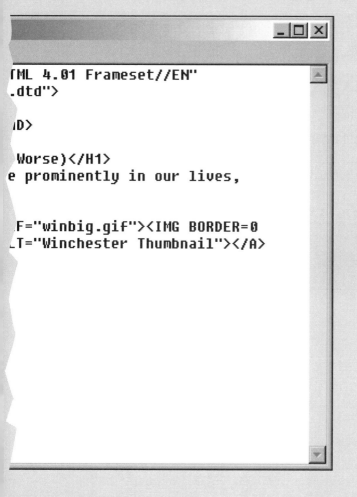

```
TML 4.01 Frameset//EN"
.dtd">

 D>

 Worse)</H1>
e prominently in our lives,


 F="winbig.gif"><IMG BORDER=0
 T="Winchester Thumbnail"></A>
```

# What You See — HTML Documents Viewed in the Browser

When you view your HTML documents as Web pages, keep in mind that different browsers display things differently. If, for example, you create a first-level heading in your HTML document, one browser may display it as 14-point Times New Roman Bold, whereas another browser may display it as 15-point Arial Bold Italic. Either way, the heading appears as bigger and bolder than normal text, but the specifics of what it looks like vary a bit from browser to browser and from user to user — it's possible that your readers might change the default fonts that their browsers use.

Even simple pages show differences in font, weight, and size — and, therefore, the amount of information on a page — if viewed in different browsers. The more complex the page designs, the more dramatic these differences can be.

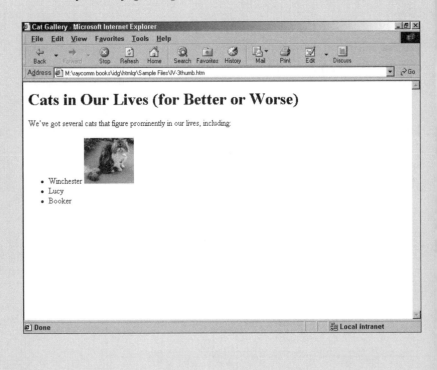

✔ View your HTML documents on as many different browsers as you can so that you have a good idea of what your readers may see. You may be surprised at the differences. Take a look at the following figure, which shows the same Web page viewed in three different browsers — Netscape Navigator at the top, Microsoft Internet Explorer at the bottom, and Lynx (text-only) sitting on the others.

✔ Use the Reload or Refresh buttons on the browser to display the latest changes to your HTML document. If you've included images or forms, you may need to use Shift+Reload (or Shift+Refresh) to make those changes.

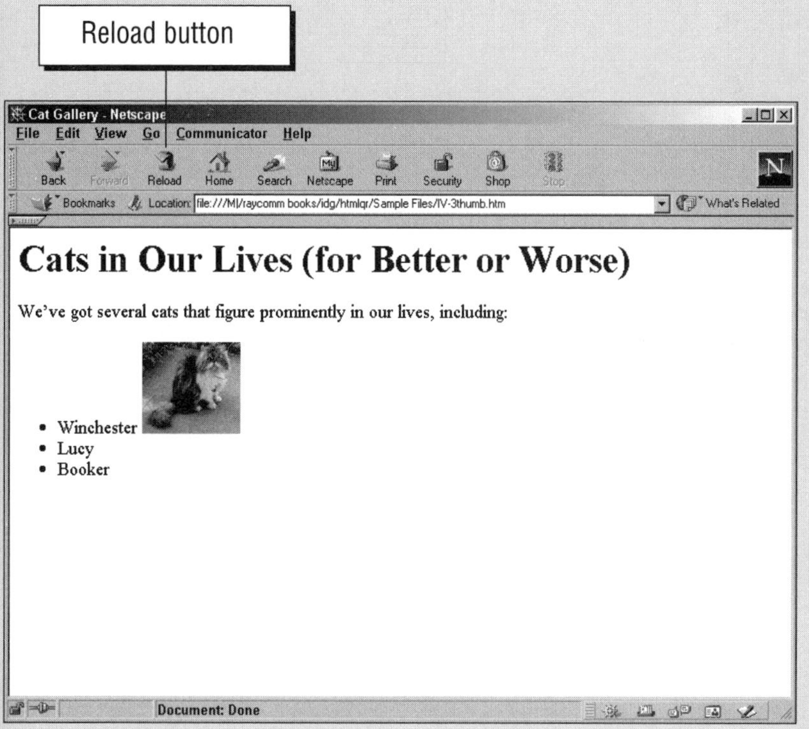

Reload button

**Cat Gallery - Netscape**

File  Edit  View  Go  Communicator  Help

Back  Forward  Reload  Home  Search  Netscape  Print  Security  Shop  Stop

Bookmarks  Location: file:///M|/raycomm books/idg/htmlqr/Sample Files/IV-3thumb.htm  What's Related

# Cats in Our Lives (for Better or Worse)

We've got several cats that figure prominently in our lives, including:

- Winchester
- Lucy
- Booker

Document: Done

5

# Tools Table

| Essential Tool | Tool Name | What It Does |
| --- | --- | --- |
| Notepad | Text editor | Provides a place to type your text and tags. Does not necessarily provide buttons or many options to automate the coding process, but does provide all the capabilities needed to enter code and save it as an HTML document. Examples of text editors and the platforms they work on are Notepad (Windows 3.x, Windows 95, Windows NT, Windows 2000, Windows ME); TeachText or Simple-Text (Macintosh); vi or pico (UNIX). |
| Internet Explorer / Netscape Navigator | Web browser | A program that interprets HTML tags and displays the documents as they should appear. Browsers are the programs that you use to view HTML documents as Web pages. Examples are Netscape Navigator, Microsoft Internet Explorer, and Lynx (used with text-only interfaces — primarily UNIX) |
| FTP Explorer | FTP software | To publish your HTML documents on the Internet, you use FTP (File Transfer Protocol) software to get your HTML documents and associated files from your computer onto a Web server. Ask your system administrator or Internet service provider (ISP) to find out what software or procedures you need to use to publish your documents. |

| Optional Tool | Tool Name | What It Does |
|---|---|---|
| Paint Shop Pro 5 | Image-editing software | Use this type of software to create images to include in your HTML document. However, a variety of clip-art libraries is available on the Internet if you'd rather use standard images than create your own. Check out Yahoo! (www.yahoo.com) and type and search for **clip art** to get started. |
| HomeSite 4.0   TextPad | Code-based HTML editor | You can use this type of editor instead of a plain old text editor. In addition to the function of a regular text editor, this type of editor provides automated capabilities such as entering tags. Good ones include: CoffeeCup, from CoffeeCup Software at www.coffeecup.com (Windows); HotDog, from Sausage Software at www.sausage.com (Windows); HomeSite, from Allaire at www.allaire.com (Windows); TEXTpad, from Helios Software at www.textpad.com (Windows); BBEdit, from Bare Bones Software at www.barebones.com (Macintosh); World Wide Web Weaver at www.miracleinc.com (Macintosh). |
| Microsoft Word   Netscape Composer | WYSIWYG | Lets you see the document approximately as it appears in a browser. In most of these editors, you don't see the tags; instead, you just click a formatting button and that action inserts the tags behind the scenes. (Netscape Composer is a good example of a commonly available and affordable (free) WYSIWYG editor, as is Microsoft Word when you use the Save As HTML option). |
| HTML Transit | WYSIWYG converter | Lets you take an existing document (or set of hundreds of documents) and turn it (or them) into an HTML document without much effort. |

# The Basics: Creating HTML Documents

HTML (HyperText Markup Language) is nothing more than the computer language (or gobbledygook, depending on your perspective) that makes World Wide Web pages:

✔ HTML is only text and doesn't actually contain images, video, or sound, although it allows you to include these things in a document.

✔ You use HTML to format a document by labeling each of its elements; you do this by applying a tag that indicates what the element is. If you show that an element is a <TITLE>, for example, the computer takes care of determining such elements as the font, font size, and emphasis (such as bold or italic). In a sense, using HTML makes creating documents easier because you don't necessarily have to choose what you want the parts of the document to look like; you must determine only what the element is.

# The Basics: Opening Your Documents

You open HTML documents and image files just as you do other files that you create:

✔ If you're creating a new document in your HTML editor or image-editing program, choose File⇨New from the File menu.

✔ If you're opening an existing document or file, choose File⇨Open, browse to the file, and click Open (or OK, depending).

# The Basics: Saving Your Documents

Regardless of the editing program you use (except for you vi users on UNIX — you know who you are), you save your document in the same way everywhere.

1. Choose File⇨Save (or Save As).

2. Choose a location.

3. Enter a filename.

4. Verify that you're saving as HTML or Text only and that you're using an .htm or .html (either one works) extension.

5. Click Save.

And remember the following:

✔ You can use a word-processing program or any number of programs that offer a Save As Text option just as you would use a plain text editor. If you use this approach, you'll be typing in the tags just as we show you in this book. You must remember to save the documents as text only — and not in the native word-processing format — or you'll get some odd gibberish at the top of the documents when you open them in a browser.

✔ You can use a word-processing program or any number of programs that offer a Save As HTML option — in effect, making your word processor perform double duty as a WYSIWYG editor. You will not actually type in the tags — you'll make the word processor do the heavy lifting, because the Save As HTML option converts your documents into HTML so that you can publish them on the Web or on an intranet. Many newer spread-sheet, database, and presentation software packages, for example, let you easily save your creation as an HTML document. Additionally, virtu-ally all current word-processing and desktop publishing software pack-ages let you save in HTML format.

# The Basics: Publishing HTML Documents

Your HTML documents are not meant to be kept as a secret — you want to do something with them, and that means putting them out on a server on the Web or on an intranet.

To publish your documents on the Internet or on most intranets, do the following:

- ✔ Find a server on which you can place your HTML documents as well as graphics and related files. Try your company or organization, your ISP, or free hosting services like www.angelfire.com or www.geocities.com.

- ✔ Get to know your system administrator. We can't know all of the details about how to use each different type of Web server and corporate setup. We suggest that you dash off an e-mail to your ISP or corporate network administrator and start asking questions. These administrators answer those questions every day, so you get the latest and greatest answer, tailored to your specific situation.

- ✔ Publish your HTML documents by putting them "out there" (on the Web or the intranet) yourself. Exactly how you do this depends on the Web server you use, but generally you transfer your files to the server with FTP software. After you transfer a document to the server, that document is available on the network.

Location line shows http:// at the beginning, indicating that the
document comes from a server.

**HTML 4.0 Characters - Netscape**

File   Edit   View   Go   Communicator   Help

Back   Forward   Reload   Home   Search   Netscape   Print   Security   Shop   Stop

Bookmarks   Location: http://www.raycomm.com/html_reference/   What's Related

## Standard Symbols (supported in previous versions of HTML)

| Symbol | Numeric | Mnemonic | Description |
|--------|---------|----------|-------------|
| " | &#34; | &quot; | quotation mark |
| & | &#38; | & | ampersand |
| < | &#60; | &lt; | less-than sign |
| > | &#62; | &gt; | greater-than sign |
|  |   |   | no-break space |
| ¡ | &#161; | &iexcl; | inverted exclamation mark |
| ¢ | &#162; | &cent; | cent sign |
| £ | &#163; | &pound; | pound sterling sign |
| ¤ | &#164; | &curren; | general currency sign |
| ¥ | &#165; | &yen; | yen sign |
| ¦ | &#166; | &brvbar; | broken (vertical) bar |
| § | &#167; | &sect; | section sign |
| ¨ | &#168; | &uml; | umlaut (dieresis) |
|  | &#169; | &copy; | copyright sign |

Document: Done

# What You Can Do: Set Up Your Personal Home Page

Most commonly, you'll use HTML documents for developing Web pages, and you'll probably start with your own. Providing basic information and links about yourself lets you get going quickly as well as (often) gives you a chance to get really creative.

## Get started by:

✔ Starting your HTML documents, Part I

✔ Adding links to your HTML documents, Part II

✔ Planning and adding images, Parts III and IV

## Advance your pages by:

✔ Experimenting with text and image alignment, Part V

✔ Experimenting with background and text colors, Part VI

## Publish your pages by:

✔ Reviewing the publishing process, Part XI

✔ Understanding publishing tools, The Big Picture "FTP Software" and "Publishing Your Documents"

# *What You Can Do: Construct an Online Newsletter*

An informational Web page (or online newsletter) provides information about a company, product, service, or family, as well as any other details the publisher might want to offer.

## Get started by:

✔ Planning your Web site content and organization, Part XI

✔ Starting your HTML documents, Part I

✔ Adding links to your HTML documents, Part II

✔ Planning and adding images, Parts III and IV

## Advance your pages by:

✔ Experimenting with tables, rules, breaks, and other options, Part V

✔ Experimenting with background and text colors, Part VI

✔ Discovering style sheets for formatting options, Part X

## Publish your pages by:

✔ Reviewing the publishing process, Part XI

✔ Understanding publishing tools, The Big Picture "FTP Software" and "Publishing Your Documents"

# What You Can Do: Develop an Internal Company Web Site

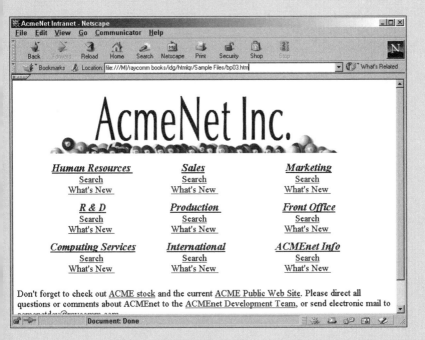

A common use for HTML documents is to publish company *intranets*, which is a smaller Web that provides information to company employees. On such intranets, employees can find out about schedule updates, corporate policies, newsletters, and similar online information.

## Get started by:

✔ Planning your Web site content and organization, Part XI

✔ Adding links to your HTML documents, Part II

## Advance your pages by:

✔ Experimenting with tables, rules, breaks, and other options, Part V

✔ Discovering forms, Part VIII

✔ Discovering frames, Part IX

✔ Discovering style sheets for formatting options, Part X

## Publish your pages by:

✔ Reviewing the publishing process, Part XI

✔ Understanding publishing tools, The Big Picture "FTP Software" and "Publishing Your Documents"

# Creating an HTML Page

The moment has come — off into the world of HTML we go!

Part I focuses on the formalities (*a.k.a.,* the boring stuff) and the fundamentals (*a.k.a.,* the fun stuff) of HTML 4.0 and 4.01. Knowing how to use these things is necessary for developing good, solid HTML pages — not to mention HTML pages that work. Unfortunately, we can't offer many shortcuts in this section; you'll probably find, however, that after you master HTML, you can whip this stuff out fairly quickly.

Before you start, you may want to review some of the terms introduced in The Big Picture of this book.

If you haven't already, go ahead and open your text editor and browser so that you can try out the examples we provide. The examples help you begin to put in tags and set up your first HTML document.

## In this part . . .

About Text and Tags . . . . . . . . . . . . . . . . . . . . . . . . . . . 18
Including HTML Structure Tags  . . . . . . . . . . . . . . . 20
Using Basic HTML Tags . . . . . . . . . . . . . . . . . . . . . . 24

## *About Text and Tags*

HTML documents basically contain the following three things:

- ✔ Text that you're working with

- ✔ Tags that determine document elements such as headings, lists, and paragraphs

- ✔ Tags that insert other objects, such as images, style sheets, sounds, little programs called applets, and movies (although many of these are outside the scope of this book)

You don't generally — at least as you're starting out — need to concern yourself with formatting text or making sure that it looks good. The browser interprets the HTML and does all that for you. Instead, you focus on accurately entering the text and tags.

You use the HTML tags that we describe in this part in pairs — one tag goes before the text, and the other tag goes after the text, as in the following example:

```
<TAG>whatever your text is</TAG>
```

- ✔ The first tag (the *opening tag*) indicates the beginning of a tag that you're applying to some of the text in your document.

- ✔ The second tag (the *closing tag*) indicates the end of a tag that you're applying.

The tags affect everything between the opening and closing tag.

Opening and closing tags are generally identical, except that the closing tag has a forward slash (/) before the tag name. The tag name is always exactly the same in the opening and closing tags.

Sometimes opening tags also include an *attribute*, which is just an additional bit of information that further specifies information such as color, alignment, or the text that should appear to describe an image. So, in such a case, an attribute appears in the initial tag, as follows:

```
<TAG ATTRIBUTE="More Info">whatever your text
is</TAG>
```

Make sure that you include the forward slash (/) in the closing tag (but don't include the attribute). If you don't, the browser doesn't know that you want to end the style that the tag indicates. And more than likely, the style you applied goes on and on and on until the browser finds a closing tag. We suggest that you go ahead and enter both the initial and closing tags at the same time. That way, you don't forget that essential closing tag.

Also, make sure that you do not include an extra space between the angle brackets and the text of the opening or closing tag. Extra space can confuse older, less-sophisticated browsers.

HTML tags are *case insensitive,* which means that you can type the tags by using either UPPERCASE letters, lowercase letters, or BoTh. We recommend, however, that you type the tags in all caps; typing the tags in all caps helps you differentiate between the tags and text, particularly after your HTML document becomes pages and pages long.

Make sure that you type the text between the tags so that the text is capitalized just as you want it to appear.

## Formatting text

Browsers disregard all formatting that's not incorporated by using *markup tags.* For example, they ignore extra spaces in the HTML document or blank lines that you use to move things down the page. As a result, the extra spaces, lines, or tabs that you put in don't affect your document's appearance.

You, for example, can type your line as follows:

```
<TAG>hill of beans information</TAG>
```

Or you can type the line like this:

```
<TAG>
hill of beans information
</TAG>
```

Or even like the following example:

```
<TAG>
hill
        of
beans
information
</TAG>
```

Any way that you type the tags and text, the result is the same.

If you work with HTML documents frequently, you find that spacing things out and being creative with indentations helps you find your place more easily.

## Nesting tags

In many cases, you may want to nest tags inside other tags. *Nesting tags* simply means enclosing tags within tags. By nesting tags, you apply multiple tags to the same bit of text.

Suppose that you want to make text both bold and italic. You can't achieve this effect by using only one tag — there isn't a "BOLD-n-ITALICS HERE" tag. Instead, you nest one tag inside the other, as the following example shows:

```
<B><I>more hill of beans information</I></B>
```

***See also*** the section "Emphasizing text," later in this part, for information about the `<B>` and `<I>` tags.

Notice that the tag that appears first (in this case, the bold tag) also appears last. If a tag starts first, it ends last. If a tag is right beside the text on the front end, it's right beside the text on the back end as well.

You can achieve the same effect by switching the order that you start the tags — as in the following line:

```
<I><B>more hill of beans information</B></I>
```

Notice that this example starts with the italic tag and nests the bold tags within the italic tags. Again, which tag you apply first doesn't matter, as long as you nest them as described.

# Including HTML Structure Tags

Now we move into a group of HTML tags that you use in every HTML document that you create. The first tags in this group are *structure tags* (so named because they define and describe a document's structure). Structure tags are similar to the key to a map. Although most structure tags do not generally affect the appearance of the document or the information contained within the document, they do help some browsers and HTML-editing programs identify document characteristics.

A couple of these tags also are defined as required parts of a valid HTML document by the people who make the HTML rules (the W3 Consortium, at www.w3.org, in case you're interested). The remaining structure tags are strongly recommended.

Few browsers or HTML editors actually require structure tags to open and display the HTML document. Because you don't know the types of browsers that your users may have, however, we also recommend that you include these tags in every HTML document you create. You may create a cool document that's useless if your user can't access it. If you don't want to put structure tags in all the time, make sure that you put them in your résumé or in anything else important.

For most HTML documents, you use five structure tags, which we list in the following table and describe in the following sections.

| HTML Tag | Purpose | Use in Pairs? |
|---|---|---|
| `<!DOCTYPE HTML PUBLIC "-//W3C//DTD HTML 4.01 Frameset//EN" "http://www.w3.org/TR/html4/frameset.dtd">` | Identifies document as an HTML document and specifies HTML version. Mandatory in all HTML documents. | No |
| `<HTML>. . .</HTML>` | Defines the document as an HTML document. | Yes |
| `<HEAD>. . .</HEAD>` | Includes introductory information about the document. | Yes |
| `<TITLE>. . .</TITLE>` | Indicates the document title. Mandatory in all HTML documents. | Yes |
| `<META NAME="KEYWORDS" CONTENT=". . .">` | Indicates keywords that describe the document. | No |
| `<META NAME="DESCRIPTION" CONTENT=". . .">` | Provides a short summary or description of the document. | No |
| `<BODY>. . .</BODY>` | Encloses all elements within the main portion of the document. | Yes |

*Note:* Before you begin, make sure that you have your browser and text editor open.

## The !DOCTYPE tag

The `!DOCTYPE` tag identifies the document as an HTML document. It appears at the top of HTML documents and notes that the document conforms to specific HTML standards — in this example, to the final HTML Version 4.01 standards. Pretty comprehensive for such a cryptic line of stuff, huh? If you use HTML editing programs, they probably put the `!DOCTYPE` tag in automatically. If they don't, however, make sure that you type the `!DOCTYPE` tag at the top of all your documents. (If you don't, nothing will break and the world won't end. But better safe than sorry, right?)

Suppose that you want to create an HTML document about making a water balloon. Enter the `!DOCTYPE` tag as follows:

```
<!DOCTYPE HTML PUBLIC "-//W3C//DTD HTML 4.01
    Frameset//EN"
    "http://www.w3.org/TR/html4/frameset.dtd">
```

## The <HTML> tag

The <HTML> tag encloses everything except the !DOCTYPE tag in every document. This tag, as the name suggests, indicates that the document is HTML. If you don't specify HTML, the browser might conceivably not read the tags as tags. Instead, the browser might read the tags as text, in which case, the document looks pretty much as it does in the text editor. In short, your document looks like a traffic accident — with stuff strewn everywhere and with at least one panicked person (that's you, the person who caused the accident).

Taking the water balloon page, enter the <HTML> tags at the beginning and end of the document, as shown in the following example:

```
<!DOCTYPE HTML PUBLIC "-//W3C//DTD HTML 4.01
    Frameset//EN"
    "http://www.w3.org/TR/html4/frameset.dtd">
<HTML>
. . .all the stuff about making water
    balloons will go here eventually. . .
</HTML>
```

## The <HEAD> and <TITLE> tags

The <HEAD> tag is part of what many browsers use to identify or reference the document. For many HTML developers, the <HEAD> tag seems completely useless. Keep in mind that although this tag doesn't have a visible application for creating an HTML document, it does have a technical application — it contains information about the document that does not actually appear within the browser window.

The <TITLE> tag, one of those about-this-document bits, goes within the <HEAD> tags. This tag is required by the HTML specification to apply a title of your choice to the document. Make your title as descriptive as you can so that people can find or identify your documents more easily on the Internet.

Taking the water balloon document one more step, add the <HEAD> and <TITLE> tags as shown in the following example:

```
<!DOCTYPE HTML PUBLIC "-//W3C//DTD HTML 4.01
    Frameset//EN"
    "http://www.w3.org/TR/html4/frameset.dtd">
<HTML>
<HEAD><TITLE>Making Effective Water Balloons
</TITLE></HEAD>
. . .all the stuff about making water balloons
    will go here eventually. . .
</HTML>
```

Notice that the `<HEAD>` and `<TITLE>` tags appear immediately after the initial `<HTML>` tag.

## The <META> tag

The `<META>` tag appears in dozens of permutations and combinations, only a couple of which will have any significant effect at all on most HTML developers. These tags, cleverly positioned right alongside the `<TITLE>` between the `<HEAD>` tags, provide more about-this-document information. This meta-information fuels Internet directories (such as Lycos at `www.lycos.com`) and search services (such as AltaVista at `www.altavista.com`) because providing the information makes categorizing and finding your documents easier. Although you don't have to include these tags, you'll greatly improve your chances of being found by people "out there" if you do.

Taking the water balloon document one more step, add the `<META NAME="KEYWORDS" CONTENT="...">` and `<META NAME="DESCRIPTION" CONTENT="...">` tags, as shown in the following example:

```
<!DOCTYPE HTML PUBLIC "-//W3C//DTD HTML 4.01
    Frameset//EN"
    "http://www.w3.org/TR/html4/frameset.dtd">
<HTML>
<HEAD><TITLE>Making Effective Water Balloons
</TITLE>
<META NAME="KEYWORDS" CONTENT="water balloon
    surprise splash splat cat oops sorry
    ouch cold wet">
<META NAME="DESCRIPTION" CONTENT="This document
    provides basic instructions for developing and
    using water balloons.">
</HEAD>
. . .all the stuff about making water balloons
    will go here eventually. . .
</HTML>
```

Notice that the `<HEAD>` and `<TITLE>` tags appear immediately after the initial `<HTML>` tag.

## The <BODY> tag

The `<BODY>` tag surrounds all the information that's actually supposed to be visible to your readers — the real heart of the document. Everything you want people to see must be contained between the `<BODY>` and `</BODY>` tags.

Place the <BODY> tag just before the information that you want to put into your HTML document and then just before the closing </HTML> tag. Technically, all other tags that you use are nested between the <BODY> and </BODY> tags.

You actually begin the water balloon project by adding the <BODY> tags, as follows:

```
<!DOCTYPE HTML PUBLIC "-//W3C//DTD HTML 4.01
   Frameset//EN"
     "http://www.w3.org/TR/html4/frameset.dtd">
<HTML>
<HEAD><TITLE>Making Effective Water Balloons
</TITLE>
<META NAME="KEYWORDS" CONTENT="water balloon
   surprise splash splat cat oops sorry
   ouch cold wet">
<META NAME="DESCRIPTION" CONTENT="This document
   provides basic instructions for developing and
   using water balloons.">
</HEAD>
<BODY>
. . .all the stuff about making water balloons. . .
</BODY>
</HTML>
```

And that's all, folks! Those are the main structure tags that you use to create all your HTML documents.

**See also** Appendix A for more structure tags that you may use on occasion. Additionally, some other tags may be automatically inserted into your HTML documents by editor or conversion programs. You'll probably get to the point that you recognize these tags, but you won't have to use them unless you really want to.

Avoid some future trouble now by saving the basic HTML file (with the head, title, and body tags) under an easy-to-remember name. If you just reuse the file, you don't need to type those stinking tags again — but remember to edit the titles and descriptions as appropriate.

# Using Basic HTML Tags

Basic HTML tags are the ones that enable you to create simple, functional effects in your HTML documents. This section describes the tags necessary for making headings, paragraphs, and lists and for emphasizing and setting off text. These tags don't produce the flashiest of HTML documents; they do, however, produce effects that you use in most, if not all, your HTML documents.

You're simply applying tags to text — precisely what the text looks like to your readers depends on the browser they use, the computer system they use, the specific settings of their system, and the style sheets you might develop in Part VIII. Again, you don't necessarily have direct control over what the readers actually see. That's just the way HTML works. Go ahead and try out the examples as you read through the information.

*Note:* Before you begin, make sure that you have your browser and text editor open.

## Making headings

HTML offers you six choices in headings, labeled as ⟨H1⟩ through ⟨H6⟩. ⟨H1⟩ is the largest and boldest of the headings, and ⟨H6⟩ is the smallest and least bold (most timid?) one. You can use these headings to show a hierarchy of information (such as the headings in this book).

| HTML Tag | Effect | Use in Pairs? |
|---|---|---|
| ⟨H1⟩. . .⟨/H1⟩ | Heading 1 | Yes |
| ⟨H2⟩. . .⟨/H2⟩ | Heading 2 | Yes |
| ⟨H3⟩. . .⟨/H3⟩ | Heading 3 | Yes |
| ⟨H4⟩. . .⟨/H4⟩ | Heading 4 | Yes |
| ⟨H5⟩. . .⟨/H5⟩ | Heading 5 | Yes |
| ⟨H6⟩. . .⟨/H6⟩ | Heading 6 | Yes |

The heading tags go in pairs — for example, ⟨H1⟩. . .⟨/H1⟩. And as with all other paired tags, the text that you want to include goes between the tags. These headings look somewhat like the example shown in the following figure, as displayed in a browser.

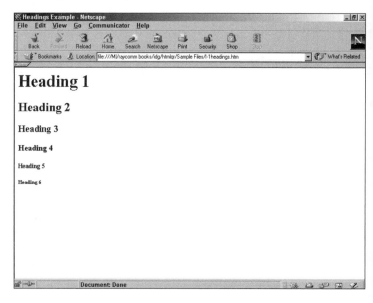

Many people have discovered that the ⟨H6⟩ tags are really small —
very, very small — and tend to use ⟨H6⟩ tags to create small text
on their pages. Unfortunately, these same people have also discovered that automatically-generated tables of contents or indexes of
their pages include their very small copyright notices and
disclaimers right up there with the important heading stuff.
Hmmm. Be careful to use heading tags only as they're intended —
for headings!

One of the first things you do is put a heading in your document. In
most cases, the first heading — the ⟨H1⟩ heading — is the name of
your document — for example, "Making Effective Water Balloons."
You enter the tags and text as shown in the following example:

```
<H1>Making Effective Water Balloons</H1>
```

Suppose that you want to use other headings within your
document. You enter these lower-level headings the same way, as
the following example demonstrates:

```
<H1>Making Effective Water Balloons</H1>
<H2>Mission Name: Cat Splats</H2>
<H3>Materials Used to Create Cat Splats</H3>
<H3>Methods Used in Cat Splat Mission</H3>
<H2>Timing the Cat Splat</H2>
<H2>Evaluating the Success of the Cat Splat
   Mission</H2>
```

The following figure shows how this code looks in a Web browser.

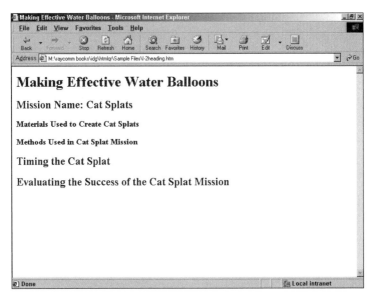

## Making paragraphs

By using HTML, you can separate information into paragraphs. The HTML paragraph tag, `<P>`, indicates the beginning and the end of a paragraph of text, respectively, as the following table shows.

| HTML Tag | Effect | Use in Pairs? |
|----------|--------|---------------|
| `<P>. . .</P>` | Indicates a paragraph. | `</P>` is optional. |

Suppose that you want to start adding information to the "Making Effective Water Balloons" document. All you do is build on your structure tags or existing information, as the following example shows:

```
<!DOCTYPE HTML PUBLIC "-//W3C//DTD HTML 4.01
    Frameset//EN"
    "http://www.w3.org/TR/html4/frameset.dtd">
<HTML>
<HEAD><TITLE>Making Effective Water Balloons
</TITLE>
</HEAD>
<BODY>
<H1>Making Effective Water Balloons</H1>
<P>
Making a water balloon is easy. . .but making
effective water balloons takes time and patience.
The result is a water balloon that does not break
```

```
in your hand, offers maximum splashing power, and
requires virtually no post-splat clean up.
</P>
</BODY>
</HTML>
```

The following figure shows the result of this HTML code in a Web browser.

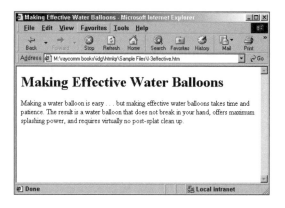

## Emphasizing text

After you write something, you may want to make some of the words within the text stand out. HTML offers several options for doing this, including emphasizing text and adding bold and italics to text. The following table describes some of these options.

| HTML Tag | Effect | Use in Pairs? |
|---|---|---|
| <EM>. . .</EM> | Adds emphasis (usually appears as italic). | Yes |
| <STRONG>. . .</STRONG> | Adds strong emphasis (usually appears as bold). | Yes |
| <B>. . .</B> | Adds boldface. | Yes |
| <I>. . .</I> | Adds italics. | Yes |

To emphasize the text in the paragraph on making effective water balloons, you can add emphasis to the word *easy* and strong emphasis to the word *effective*. You can also add boldface to *break* and italics to *maximum splashing power*. The following example demonstrates the use of these tags:

```
<!DOCTYPE HTML PUBLIC "-//W3C//DTD HTML 4.01
    Frameset//EN"
```

```
              "http://www.w3.org/TR/html4/frameset.dtd">
<HTML>
<HEAD><TITLE>Making Effective Water Balloons
</TITLE>
</HEAD>
<BODY>
<H1>Making Effective Water Balloons</H1>
<P>
Making water balloons is <EM>easy</EM>...but
making <STRONG>effective</STRONG> water balloons
takes time and patience. The result is a water
balloon that does not <B>break</B> in your hand,
offers <I>maximum splashing power</I>, and requires
virtually no post splat clean up.
</P>
</BODY>
</HTML>
```

Notice that the tags are positioned around the word or words that
you want to emphasize. The following figure shows how these
codes change the appearance of the Web page.

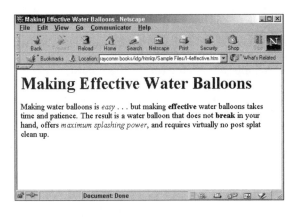

You can also add more than one kind of emphasis to a word.
Suppose that you want to add both <I> and <B> to the word *easy*.
You do so as follows:

```
<P>
Making water balloons is <I><B>easy</B></I>.
</P>
```

In this case, the <B> tags are nested inside the <I> tags. You can
also nest the <I> tags inside the <B> tags. The order in which you
nest the tags doesn't matter.

If you don't want the punctuation to appear emphasized, make sure that you place it outside the emphasis tags, as shown in the preceding example.

If possible, consider using logical formatting tags — ⟨EM⟩, ⟨STRONG⟩ — rather than the physical ones — ⟨B⟩, ⟨I⟩. Some browsers — such as the ones that read Web pages aloud for users who are visually impaired — cannot display italics or boldface. If you tell the browser to emphasize the text in any way possible (logical formatting), one browser may boldface the text, whereas others may underline the text or pronounce it with emphasis. If you just tell the browser to put something in boldface (physical formatting) but it can't, the browser ignores you and the key phrase remains unemphasized.

## Making lists

Often you may want to provide information in lists rather than in paragraphs. Providing information in lists is especially valuable in HTML documents because lists allow the reader to gather information quickly without needing to wade through paragraphs of text. And for you, the writer, making lists is an easy way to help organize your information and provide easy links to other pages. (***See also*** Part II for more information about links.)

Making lists is a two-part process. First, you must add a pair of tags to specify that the information is to appear in a list. You can specify, for example, an ordered (or numbered) list, ⟨OL⟩. . .⟨/OL⟩; or an unordered (or bulleted) list, ⟨UL⟩. . .⟨/UL⟩. You use ordered lists if you want to list things that need to go in a specific order, such as instructions. You use unordered lists if you just want to make a list of things, such as ingredients for water balloons.

Then, you must specify each line of the list, called line items. Just put the ⟨LI⟩ tag at the beginning of each line, where you want the number or bullet to be. No closing tag is required here.

Make sure that you use lists whenever possible. After a few hours of cruising around HTML pages, readers' eyes get pretty buggy, and they kinda' gloss over several paragraphs in a row. Readers still, however, read the lists. Lists are the "music-video/short-attention-span" approach to organizing information, as opposed to the "extended-essay" approach.

The following table shows the tags you use to create lists.

| HTML Tag | Effect | Use in Pairs? |
|---|---|---|
| ⟨LI⟩ | Identifies each item in a list. | No |
| ⟨OL⟩. . .⟨/OL⟩ | Specifies ordered (numbered) lists. | Yes |
| ⟨UL⟩. . .⟨/UL⟩ | Specifies unordered (bulleted) lists. | Yes |

To add an unordered (bulleted) list of materials to the "Making Effective Water Balloons" page, perform the following steps:

1. Add opening and closing `<UL>` tags where you want the list to appear, as shown in the following example:

```
<!DOCTYPE HTML PUBLIC "-//W3C//DTD HTML 4.01
   Frameset//EN"
   "http://www.w3.org/TR/html4/frameset.dtd">
<HTML>
<HEAD><TITLE>Making Effective Water
Balloons</TITLE>
</HEAD>
<BODY>
<H1>Making Effective Water Balloons</H1>
<P>
Making water balloons is <EM>easy</EM>...
but making <B>effective</B> water balloons
takes time and patience. The result is a
water balloon that does not break in your
hand, offers <I>maximum splashing power</I>,
and requires virtually no post splat clean
up.
</P>
<H2>Materials Needed</H2>
<UL>
</UL>
</BODY>
</HTML>
```

2. Add `<LI>` tags for each item, along with the text for the item, as follows:

```
<UL>
<LI>Water
<LI>Big, big balloon
<LI>Balloon ties (optional)
<LI>Second-story window
<LI>Target below window
</UL>
```

The following figure shows the results of adding these tags and text.

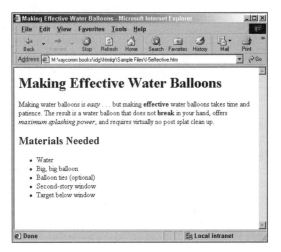

Notice that the list tags don't have <P> tags around them. If you have a list, you don't need a <P>.

To add an ordered list of instructions on how to make effective water balloons, you use the <OL> tags, as follows:

*1.* Add opening and closing <OL> tags where the list appears, as in the following example.

```
<H2>Instructions</H2>
<OL>
</OL>
```

*2.* Add <LI> tags and text for each item, as follows:

```
<H2>Instructions</H2>
<OL>
<LI>Fill balloon with water.
<LI>Tie balloon using a tie or by making a
   knot.
<LI>Go to second-story window.
<LI>Aim at spot below window.
<LI>Drop balloon.
</OL>
```

These examples appear as shown in the following figure.

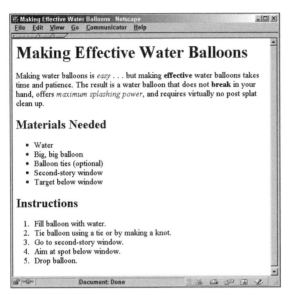

You can add attributes (extra information) to your list tags to control what the bullets look like, what kind of numbers (Roman, capital letters, regular Arabic numbers, and so on) appear, and what the starting number is for sequential lists. **See also** Appendix A for the specific attributes.

## Setting off text

Occasionally, you need to set off information from the rest of the text. HTML lets you set off text by using a number of body markup tags (listed comprehensively in Appendix A). These tags are all used in a very similar fashion, so after you've mastered one set, you're all set to use the rest of them as well.

You may, for example, have a really neat quotation to include in your page. Because longer quotations are often visibly different from the rest of the text (by virtue of indents on both sides) and might be something readers would search for within pages, you use different tags to identify the quote — the <BLOCKQUOTE>. . . </BLOCKQUOTE> tags, to be specific. This pair of tags makes the text look just like the body text but generally with an increased amount of white space in both margins.

# Spinning Your HTML Web

In this part, you see how to add anchors and links to your HTML documents. Anchors and links allow your readers to jump from place to place within your document or to other documents and files. So get ready for the wild Web of HTML.

You apply lots of tags in this section, so if initial tags, closing tags, and phrases such as "applying markup tags to your document" are unfamiliar, you may want to turn back to Part I for more information about HTML basics.

## In this part . . .

About Links . . . . . . . . . . . . . . . . . . . . . . . . . . . . . . . . 36
About Anchors . . . . . . . . . . . . . . . . . . . . . . . . . . . . . . 40
Making Your First Links . . . . . . . . . . . . . . . . . . . . . . 41
Making Links within Documents . . . . . . . . . . . . . . . 44

# *About Links*

When you create HTML documents, you create documents that users can read by *linking* from topic to topic — that is, jumping from page to page and from topic to topic instead of reading linearly, as in a novel. *Links* (or *hyperlinks* or *hot spots*) are places that users can select to access other topics, documents, or *Web sites* (collection of HTML documents).

As you build your HTML documents, think about how you want your documents to link together. As a rule, you should create several short HTML documents rather than one long document. Short documents are easier for your readers to follow and are, therefore, more likely to be read. You can then link these shorter documents into a single cohesive set of documents (that is, a Web site).

If you expect to be revising and updating the information frequently, however, or if your readers intended to print the documents and refer to them on hard copy (tree killer!), you should use fewer, but longer, documents to reduce your headaches as well as those of your readers.

To create a link, you need the following two things:

- **A URL (or Uniform Resource Locator):** This is just an address on the Web.

- **An anchor tag:** Marks the link in a Web page. (You read more about these later in this part.)

## About URLs

A *URL* (pronounced You-Are-Ell), or *Uniform Resource Locator,* is a fancy way of saying an address for information on the Internet. If you hear URL, just think "address" or "location." URLs differ based on how specific you need to be.

URLs can be *absolute* (complete) or *relative* (partial), as described in the following list:

- If you're creating a document that you want to publish on the Internet, you use an absolute URL so that anyone — anywhere in the world — on the Internet can find the page.

- If you're creating links to other files within the same folder or on the same server, you need to provide only a relative URL. Remember that you're already in the same directory (or folder or general vicinity) as the file to which you're linking.

*See also* "Absolute and relative URLs," later in this part.

All HTML documents can use URLs to link to other information. URLs, in turn, can point to many different things, such as HTML documents, other sites on the Internet, or even images and sound files.

URLs are *case sensitive.* On some computers, typing a filename such as `Kitten.html` is very different from typing `kitten.html`. If you create a filename that uses special capitalization (instead of, say, using all lowercase characters), you must use this same capitalization the same way every time you link to the document. (It'd be easier for you and your readers to just use lowercase.)

## Anatomy of URLs

If you're not used to them, URLs can be pretty odd looking. Each part of a URL has a built-in specific meaning, however, much like each part of your home address. The street address "12 Fritter Lane, Apartment G, Santa Clara, CA 95051," for example, provides a postal carrier with essential and complete information — the specific apartment in a specific building on a specific street in a specific town in a specific state in a specific ZIP Code. Specifically.

URLs work the same way by providing a browser with all the parts it needs to locate information. A URL consists of the *protocol indicator,* the *hostname,* and the *directory name* and/or *filename.* The following (fictitious) URL is an example of an absolute URL:

`http://cat.feline.org/fur/fuzzy.html`

Here's a description of each URL part:

- `http://` **portion** *(protocol indicator):* Tells the server how to send the information. The protocol indicator is the standard used by Web servers and browsers that lets them talk to each other. If you're creating HTML documents, people point to them by using `http://` as the protocol indicator. You might notice that the `http://` protocol indicator often is omitted by publications (like this one), both for space and because most URLs (at least those published in the media) tend to be `http://` type URLs.

  *Note:* Even though you can leave the `http://` off the URL in casual usage, you must include it when linking to another Web site, as described later.

  *See also* Part VII for more information about servers.

- `cat.feline.org` **portion** *(hostname):* Specifies a computer on the Internet. If you publish an HTML document, you're placing it on a computer that "serves" the document to anyone who knows the correct URL. This computer has an address that's common to all documents that it stores. The server thus "hosts" all these documents and makes them accessible to users.

To obtain the hostname of the server on which you place your files, check with your system administrator.

✔ `fur` portion (*directory name*): You may not need to show a directory name, or you may have several that represent directories inside directories (or folders inside folders). If you have an account with an Internet service provider, your directory name may also begin with a ~ and your user name, yielding something such as `http://cat.feline.org/~lucy/`, assuming, of course, that `lucy` is the account name.

✔ `fuzzy.html` portion (*name of file located on the host computer*): Sometimes you don't need to provide a filename — the server simply gives out the default file in the directory. The default filenames are usually one of three: `index.html`, `default.html`, or `homepage.html`, depending on which kind of Web server the files are located. The filename is like many other files; it contains a name (`fuzzy`) and an extension (`.html`).

Sometimes URLs have a hostname with a port number at the end (for example, `cat.feline.org:80`). This number gives the server more precise information about the URL. If you see a URL with a number, just leave the number on the URL. If you don't see a number, don't worry about it.

Try to avoid creating directory names or filenames with spaces or other unusual characters. Stay with letters (uppercase and lowercase), numbers, underscores (_), periods (.), or plus signs (+). Some servers have problems with odd characters. And if you do use any capitalization in your filenames, you must also use the same capitalization in any links pointing to those files because some servers require consistent capitalization. Our advice? Stay away from capitalization — just use lowercase letters.

## Absolute and relative URLs

As we mention earlier in this part, links in Web pages use two different types of URLs: absolute URLs and relative URLs. Each of these types of URLs has a specific purpose and uses specific components, as the following list describes:

✔ **Absolute URLs:** These give the full address of something on the Internet. They include the protocol indicator, hostname, and directory name/filenames. You use absolute URLs to indicate any location on the Internet.

Keep in mind that pointing people to Internet locations requires as much information as you can provide, just as you'd provide very detailed information to an out-of-town friend who's driving to your apartment. You'd provide, for example, the state, city, building number, and apartment number (unless, of course, you want that friend to get lost). Similarly, you need to provide as complete a URL as possible — including the protocol indicator — so that people around the world can find your Web site.

✔ **Relative URLs:** These don't contain a complete address, but they can still provide all the information you need to link to other documents. A relative URL usually contains only the last part of the absolute URL — the directory name (possibly) and the filename. You use relative URLs to link to locations within the same folder or same group of folders.

To go back to the postal address analogy, if you're giving a local friend directions to your apartment, you'd probably just provide the street address, building, and apartment. The city and state are implicit. In the same way, a relative URL implies the missing information based on the location of the file containing the relative URL. The browser infers the missing information from the location of the document containing the link.

A relative URL that starts with a slash (/) is a server-relative URL — you can just add the name of the server to the beginning of the URL, and you get the complete URL. A relative URL that doesn't start with a slash may not be relative to the server, so because the browser may need more information about the file location, adding the server name doesn't produce a complete URL.

Huh? How about an example: Suppose that in the `http://cat.feline.org/fur/fuzzy.html` document, you want to link users to more information within the same folder (say, information about kittens). Instead of typing the entire URL again, plus `kitten.html`, you use `kitten.html` for the URL in the current document. The computer understands that if you include an incomplete URL in a link, the rest of the information is derived from the location of the file from which you're linking.

Also, within the `fuzzy.html` document, you may have pointers to other documents using partial URLs on the same server — for example, `/colors/calico.html` and `/colors/tortoiseshell.html`. The `calico.html` and `tortoiseshell.html` files are located within the `colors` directory. These files are server-relative — they all have the same server. So you can add `http://cat.feline.org` to the beginning and have an accurate, absolute URL.

Of course, you need the absolute URL only if you're linking from another location or if you're entering the URL directly in your browser. If you're linking from another document located on the same server, you can just use the relative URL in your document.

Relative URLs are great for weaving a whole web of HTML documents with all kinds of interconnections. You can put your documents on a server or give them to someone else for installation on another computer, and the links among the documents continue to work. As a matter of fact, unless you really need to use an absolute URL (to point to an entirely different Internet site, for example), don't. Relative URLs are just more practical.

Check out the following figure, which shows how absolute URLs and relative URLs work.

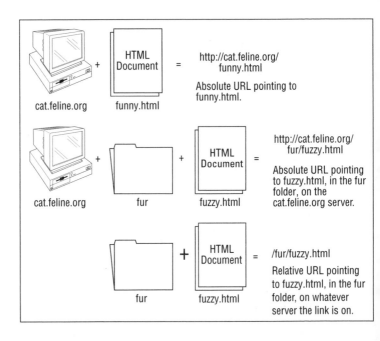

## *About Anchors*

The linking process begins with anchors; this term is just a fancy way of saying links. (We call them anchors because the tag is ⟨A⟩.)

Anchor tags are generally used with one of the following two attributes:

✔ HREF: Allows users to jump from one bit of information to another — either to material within the same Web site or to other material out on the Internet. These tags create the hyperlinks.

✔ NAME: Labels a spot within a document. That spot can then be part of a URL so that readers can jump directly to it. The NAME anchor is useful in long documents that users must otherwise scroll through. If NAME anchors and links to them are present, users can jump to specific information and don't need to wade through pages of material.

| HTML Tag or Attribute | Effect | Use in Pairs? |
|---|---|---|
| `<A>...</A>` | Marks anchor. | Yes |
| `HREF="..."` | Indicates where to jump. | No |
| `NAME="..."` | Identifies an internal label. | No |

# Making Your First Links

Links are the connections to other material within or among HTML documents. Links are visible as (often blue) text that you select as you're surfing the Web. (After you've linked to a document, the link often appears in a different color to indicate that you've already been there.) The next three sections show you how to link to other documents within your site, link to HTML documents "out there" on the Web, and link to other information on the Internet. For now, you work with the `<A>` tag's HREF attribute.

## Linking to documents within your site

Here you start with plain text and build your first hypertext link. We recommend that you work with two, preferably small, HTML documents so that you can link from one to the other and back again. Practicing linking is much more difficult if you work with just one document.

**Note:** Before beginning the example in this section, open your text editor and browser. While trying these examples, you should also have available a basic HTML document, such as the following:

```
<!DOCTYPE HTML PUBLIC "-//W3C//DTD HTML 4.01
    Frameset//EN"
    "http://www.w3.org/TR/html4/frameset.dtd">
<HTML><HEAD><TITLE>Cats</TITLE></HEAD>
<BODY>
</BODY>
</HTML>
```

Now follow these steps:

*1.* Enter `Cats are funny` between the `<BODY>` tags, as the following example shows:

```
<BODY>
Cats are funny.
</BODY>
```

*2.* Apply the anchor tags to funny, as follows, to make that word the anchor (the part that your readers click to link to something else):

```
Cats are <A>funny</A>.
```

*3.* Add an attribute (`HREF=`, in this case) to link to another document, as follows:

```
Cats are <A HREF="funny.html">funny</A>.
```

`HREF=` is the attribute that specifies which document appears after your readers click the anchor. And `funny.html` is the name of the document to which you are linking.

In this case, `funny.html` is a file in the same directory or folder as the document that you're building.

If you want to link the same bit of text to a file within a new folder, just add the necessary folder information, as follows:

```
Cats are <A HREF="newfolder/funny.html">funny</A>.
```

Notice the slash. Its function is to separate the directory or folder name and the filename. The slash is a required element of a pathname.

To link the same bit of text to a file in a folder somewhere else on the server, you can make a server-relative URL by adding a slash and a folder name, as follows:

```
Cats are <A
HREF="/folderonserver/funny.html">funny</A>.
```

If you create one of these URLs, you must check to make sure that it really is a server-relative URL. If you can't add the server name to the beginning and make it work, don't put a slash at the beginning of the relative URL.

## Linking to pages out on the Web

To create links to other documents on the Internet, follow the same procedure as with other links, but include the complete URL in the `HREF` attribute.

To make a link from the word cats to a completely different address, use the following example, starting with the following basic HTML document.

*Note:* Before beginning, open your text editor and browser.

```
<!DOCTYPE HTML PUBLIC "-//W3C//DTD HTML 4.01
    Frameset//EN"
    "http://www.w3.org/TR/html4/frameset.dtd">
<HTML><HEAD><TITLE>Cats</TITLE></HEAD>
<BODY>
</BODY>
</HTML>
```

Use the following steps to add a link to a document at another location:

*1.* Type Cats are funny between the <BODY> tags, as follows:

```
<BODY>
Cats are funny.
</BODY>
```

*2.* Add the following anchor tags:

```
<A>Cats</A> are funny.
```

*3.* Add the HREF attribute to link to a sample (fictitious) Web site about cats, as follows:

```
<A HREF="http://cats.com/home.html">Cats</A>
    are funny.
```

You can also link to files from a regular http:// type address. If, for example, you have a Word document that you want people to be able to download from your Web site, you can put in a link such as the following:

```
<A HREF="catjokes.doc">Download original cat
    stories here</A>.
```

Or you could use an absolute URL, as follows:

```
<A HREF="http://cat.feline.org/furry/catjokes.doc">
    Download original cat stories here</A>.
```

Then all you need to do is upload the catjokes.doc file to the server at the same time that you upload your HTML document to the server.

As you're making anchors, try to avoid using "Click here." By the time they see your page, your readers have probably figured out that they need to click links to go from one place to another.

### Linking to other stuff on the Internet

Just as you can link to HTML documents or images or files on the Internet by including the right URL, you can also link to other types of information (such as discussion groups or file archives) on the Internet. All kinds of other protocols (the language that computers use to transfer information) are in use.

For example, if you see or hear of neat material on the Internet that's available through an FTP (File Transfer Protocol) site (a source for data on the Internet), you can link that material into your document.

Suppose that your best friend found a collection of cat jokes at an FTP site on the Internet. You can simply copy the URL from your friend. The URL may look something like `ftp://humor.central.org/jokes/animals/cats.zip`. You can put that URL into your document as shown here.

```
A collection of <A HREF="ftp://humor.central.org/
    jokes/animals/cats.zip"> cat jokes</A> is good
    to have.
```

## Making Links within Documents

Making links to places within an HTML document requires a little more work than creating links to other documents. On regular links to other documents or to documents on other servers, you just point to a computer and a file. If you're going to point to a place within a document that you're creating, however, you must also identify the targets to which you intend to link.

### Making internal links

An internal link points to a specific location within a document. Internal links work well if you have a long HTML document that really doesn't lend itself to being split into different files. If you're dealing with one of these long documents, you can use internal links to point from one place to another within the same document. As a result, readers don't need to scroll through pages of information; they can just link to a place (defined by a special anchor) within the document.

Within the `kitten.html` file, you may have a long list of favorite kitten names along with a description of the names' origins. You can enable readers to jump right to the "W" names without needing to scroll through the "A" through "V" names. The following URL points directly to the "w" anchor within the kitten.html file:

```
kitten.html#w
```

The relative URL could also be written as follows:

```
fur/kitten.html#w
```

or

```
/fur/kitten.html#w
```

Or you could write the address as the following absolute URL:

```
http://cat.feline.org/fur/kitten.html#w
```

## Marking internal targets

Developing anchors to permit links to points within a document is very similar to creating the links themselves. You use the NAME= attribute that we mention in the preceding section. These targets are called name anchors, or internal targets.

(In the preceding — and hypothetical — example, the author of kitten.html inserted name anchors for all 26 A–Z headings, just so that you can link to them.)

For the following example, imagine that you have a heading within your document called "Funny Cats I've Known."

*Note:* Before beginning, open your text editor and browser. You should also have a basic HTML document such as the following one available while you try these examples:

```
<!DOCTYPE HTML PUBLIC "-//W3C//DTD HTML 4.01
    Frameset//EN"
    "http://www.w3.org/TR/html4/frameset.dtd">
<HTML><HEAD><TITLE>Cats</TITLE></HEAD>
<BODY>
<H2>Funny Cats I've Known</H2>
General information about the cats would be here.
</BODY>
</HTML>
```

Now follow these steps to include the anchor:

*1.* Include an anchor, as follows:

```
<H2><A>Funny</A> Cats I've Known</H2>
```

*2.* Insert the NAME= attribute, as follows:

```
<H2><A NAME="funny">Funny</A> Cats I've
    Known</H2>
```

This anchor doesn't show up in the browser view of your document, but you know it's there.

If you're preparing HTML documents that someone may use for reference or to which other people may be interested in linking their pages, we suggest inserting some logical NAME= anchors. Even if you don't think you can use them, you'll find that putting them in while you're creating your page is easier than putting them in later.

If you want to link directly to the funny cats section of your document from within the same document, you can include a link to #funny, as follows:

```
<A HREF="#funny">Funny cats</A> are here.
```

The #funny anchor to which you want to link, for example, may be in the cats.html file on the server called cat.feline.org. You just create a URL that looks as follows:

```
http://cat.feline.org/cats.html#funny
```

Your friends and admirers can then set up links to your funny cats section:

```
Boy, you know, those <A HREF="http://
    cat.feline.org/cats.html#funny">funny cats
    </A> are something else.
```

# Using Images in Your Web Pages

Part III focuses on using images (or pictures or graphics) in your Web pages. We tell you all about finding and including images, and we make some recommendations about how you should (and should not) use images in your Web pages.

If you're a creative type and want to make your own images, you can — you just need to be comfortable using an image-editing or paint program. If you consider yourself artistically impaired, however, you can always use existing images from the Internet or commercial clip art archives.

*See also* Part I before beginning this part if you need a quick recap of basic tags. Most of the examples in this part include only the tags and attributes discussed in this part and do not include structure or body tags.

*See also* Part IV for details about using images as links, thumbnails, and creating imagemaps (those neat clickable images).

## In this part . . .

Adding Images . . . . . . . . . . . . . . . . . . . . . . . . . . . . . 48
Addressing Image Download Speed . . . . . . . . . . . 57
Controlling Image Alignment . . . . . . . . . . . . . . . . . 60

# *Adding Images*

Adding images to your HTML documents is just as straightforward as the basic link and text tags are. (Whenever we talk about adding images, we mean including all sorts of pictures, drawings, or diagrams in your HTML documents.)

You can include images with either *GIF* (usually pronounced *jiff*), *JPG* (pronounced *jay-peg*), or PNG (pronounced *ping*) file formats. These formats are compressed, so they take up minimal disk space and downloading time. You'll choose which format to use based on the image itself:

✔ Choose GIF images for line drawings, images with only a few colors, images that should blend into the background (*see* "Creating transparent images" later in this part), or animated images. GIF remains a popular file format because all graphical browsers can interpret and display them and because transparent images are far spiffier than the regular kind.

✔ Choose JPG images for photographic images or images with fancy shading. Consider using the JPG file format only if you're including a photograph or another image that takes up a lot of disk space. Although not quite all browsers can interpret this format (*most* can, however), JPG files are considerably smaller in terms of disk space and, therefore, don't take f-o-r-e-v-e-r to download to your readers' browsers.

✔ Choose PNG images if you have photographic or complex images and you know your readers will be using newer browsers: Microsoft Internet Explorer 4.0 and Netscape Navigator 4.03 or newer.

Adding images isn't too complicated — just include an ⟨IMG⟩ tag and the SRC="..." attribute, pointing to a valid URL (either absolute or relative) for your image.

*See also* Part II for more information about absolute and relative URLs.

The following table shows some of the common image-related tags and attributes.

| HTML Tag or Attribute | Effect | Use in Pairs? |
|---|---|---|
| ⟨IMG SRC="..."⟩ | Inserts an image. | No |
| ALT="..." | Specifies text to display if image isn't displayed. | No |
| BORDER=n | Controls thickness of border around an image in pixels. | No |

The following example shows you how to add an image to your document.

***Note:*** Before beginning, make sure that you have your browser and text editor open and ready to create a new document. Or you can apply this information to an existing document. You should also have an image available to use in the document.

To include an image in your document, follow these steps:

*1.* Start your HTML page.

Start with the following sample of HTML code:

```
<!DOCTYPE HTML PUBLIC "-//W3C//DTD HTML 4.01
   Frameset//EN"
   "http://www.w3.org/TR/html4/frameset.dtd">
<HTML>
<HEAD><TITLE>Cat Gallery</TITLE></HEAD>
<BODY>
<H1>Cats in Our Lives (for Better or Worse)
   </H1>
<P>We've got several cats that figure
   prominently in our lives, including:</P>
<UL>
<LI>Winchester
<LI>Lucy
<LI>Booker
</UL>
</BODY>
</HTML>
```

*2.* Add the <IMG> tag wherever you want your image to appear, as in the following example:

```
<P>We've got several cats that figure
   prominently in our lives, including:</P>
<IMG>
```

*3.* Add the SRC= attribute to provide the address of the image, as the following example shows.

(The image we're using is called winchest.jpg, and it's located in the same folder as our HTML document.)

```
<IMG SRC="winchest.jpg">
```

*4.* Add the ALT= attribute to describe the image, just in case the viewer can't view (or chooses not to view) the image, as follows:

```
<IMG SRC="winchest.jpg" ALT="Winchester the
   Cat">
```

The resulting Web page looks like the following figure.

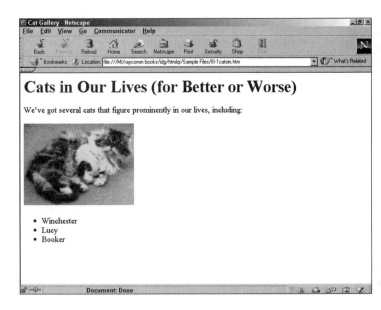

Technically, you don't *have to* provide the ALT= text (which stands for *alternative text*) with the image; however, doing so is a good idea. Sometimes people use browsers — including read-aloud browsers for the visually impaired — that can't display images.

Many people also commonly stop their browsers from showing images so that they don't need to wait for the images to copy to their computer over a slow modem connection.

By using alternative text, you tell them what they're missing instead of making them guess. As a bonus, many browsers use the alternative text for those cute little pop-up blurbs that appear when you hover your mouse over the image.

The following figure shows an example of how the alternative text may look to readers viewing the same page without the images.

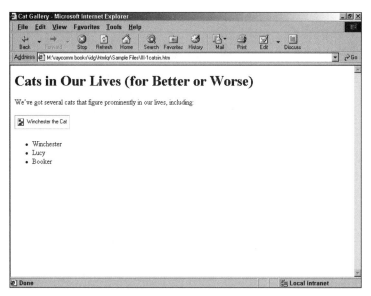

## Creating images for HTML documents

Creating images for your HTML documents isn't really any more difficult than creating other images. You draw/format/edit/tweak the image and save it in a specific file format for use on the Web.

As you're creating images for HTML documents, keep in mind that some colors work better than others. Check the following section, "Choosing colors carefully," for information about choosing colors for use in HTML documents.

The following example shows you how to get images in the correct formats for use in HTML documents.

*Note:* You need to be familiar with how to use a drawing or image-editing program to create images. You could use anything from Adobe Photoshop to Microsoft PowerPoint to the drawing tools in your word-processing program to develop images. Whichever program(s) you choose, you need to make sure that at least one of them can save images in GIF or JPG format.

To create images appropriate for use in HTML documents, follow these steps:

*1.* Create an image that you want to use in your HTML document.

*2.* In the program you use to create the image, click File⇨Save As (or on File⇨Export or something similar) to save the image as a GIF, JPG, or PNG image.

*3.* Type a name and a location in your Save As dialog box.

Make sure that the image type you select is either GIF, JPG, or PNG and that the location is the same as your HTML documents (for ease of linking).

If your favorite image-editing program doesn't save in GIF, JPG, or PNG formats, you can try either of the following approaches:

✔ Save the image as a TIF image and import the file into a program that can save it in the format you want. Paint Shop Pro for Windows, GraphicConverter for Macintosh, and xv for UNIX are some possible candidates.

✔ Copy the image from the image-editing program (by selecting the image and choosing Edit⇨Copy from the menu bar), and then paste the image into the other program, the one that can save in the correct format (by choosing Edit⇨Paste from that program's menu bar).

This second procedure also works well if you have an image-editing program such as Photoshop or Paint Shop Pro (which can save in the right format) but you're more comfortable being creative in a different program, such as PowerPoint (which saves slides, but not individual images, in the correct format).

## Choosing colors carefully

Good color choices are ones that look good in practically any browser and operating system and display resolution configuration. That is, they show up clearly, not splotchy or mottled. Unfortunately, color involves more than meets the eye.

The following information about choosing colors applies not only to image colors but also to background colors (which we cover in Part V).

As you're choosing colors, keep in mind that not all colors are created equally. Some colors don't show up at all in readers' browsers. If you choose a color from the 16.7 million-color palette, for example, and your readers' browsers are set to only 256 colors, the color you choose may not show up crisp and clear (unless it's one of the 256). For that matter, even if you choose a color from the 256-color palette, the color could show up splotchy (a condition technically called *dithered*) on many readers' screens.

To figure out which colors to use, you should first know how colors are described. For the Web, you specify colors with an RGB (Red-Green-Blue) number. By using three numbers (either three decimal numbers or three two-digit hex numbers), you can specify the amounts of red, green, and blue to create any one of about 16.7 million colors. By mixing the levels of RGB, you can create any color you want.

So which colors are best to use in HTML documents? Colors that are standard across all platforms and that look good even at lower color resolutions. How do you know which ones? Fortunately, you can find a list and color samples on the Cheat Sheet in the front of this book. Or just choose colors with the values from the tables in the following sections. By using these values to choose colors (pick one number from each column to create the RGB number), you stand the best chance of having the colors show up clearly in just about any browser.

**If your image-editing software uses hexadecimal numbers:** The *hexadecimal numbering system* (*hex*) provides you with the same values as the decimal system does, but hex uses 16 digits instead of 10. The digits for hex are 0–9 and the letters A–F in place of the numbers 10–15. By using two hex digits (##), you can specify a number between 0 (or 00 in hex) and 255 (FF in hex).

The following table provides values you can use if your image-editing software uses hexadecimal numbers. Use the following table as you would a Chinese restaurant menu (one from column Red, one from column Green, and one from column Blue) to choose six-digit color numbers. You also use the hexadecimal numbers for specifying colors within your HTML documents (say, for the background). *See also* Part VI for details about specifying background and text colors.

*Hexadecimal Color Selections*

| Red | Green | Blue |
|-----|-------|------|
| 00 | 00 | 00 |
| 33 | 33 | 33 |
| 66 | 66 | 66 |
| 99 | 99 | 99 |
| CC | CC | CC |
| FF | FF | FF |

You may, for example, choose hexadecimal #336699 or #CC00CC or #FFFFFF to be reasonably sure that the color looks pure on most displays. The hex number FF0000 is Red, 00FF00 is Green, and 0000FF is Blue. White is equal amounts of each color (because you're working with light), so you can create it by choosing FFFFFF. Black, on the other hand, uses no color at all and is 000000.

**If your image-editing software uses decimal numbers:** The follow-ing table provides values you can use if your image-editing software uses decimal RGB numbers to set colors. Again, think Chinese restaurant menu — take a number from column Red, then a number from column Green, and the final number from column Blue.

| Decimal Color Selections Red | Green | Blue |
|---|---|---|
| 0 | 0 | 0 |
| 51 | 51 | 51 |
| 102 | 102 | 102 |
| 153 | 153 | 153 |
| 204 | 204 | 204 |
| 255 | 255 | 255 |

You may, for example, choose an RGB color such as decimal 0, 51, 102 — or perhaps 204, 153, 255 — to make fairly sure that the color looks good on displays that show only 256 colors. The RGB color 0, 0, 0 is black, for example, whereas 255, 0, 0 is red, and 255, 255, 255 is white.

## Borrowing images

Borrowing images from other Web pages helps provide you with ideas and gives you materials that you can use to practice includ-ing images in your documents.

Of course, we don't recommend using other people's images in your public Web pages (because of copyright laws and because doing so is just plain wrong). Remember that whoever created the image you're borrowing holds the copyright to it. Don't just take the image and use it in your own documents. Of course, if the image is clearly labeled as one that you're free to use in your own pages and you know that the individual or group giving permission has the right to give that permission, you're in the clear.

A number of very good sites on the Internet offer clip art or Web art that's free for noncommercial use. Check out Yahoo! (at www.yahoo.com) by typing and searching for **clip art**. You'll find all you could ever use.

The following procedure shows you how to borrow images from other documents on the Web.

*Note:* Before beginning, make sure that you have your browser open.

To borrow images off the Web, follow these steps:

1. Find an HTML document that you like on the Web.

   (You can do this step as often as you want, so don't be too picky.)

2. Using the right mouse button, click the image that you want to copy.

   A pop-up menu appears providing several options. (*Note:* If you're a Macintosh user, you just click and hold the mouse button for a couple of seconds.)

3. Choose the Save Image As option from the pop-up menu.

   (Although the option in your program may not be worded exactly as it is here, it should be similar.)

4. Type a name and a location in your Save As dialog box, and click Save.

   Again, you make your life easier if you choose the same location (folder) as that in which you keep your HTML documents.

## Creating transparent images

A transparent image is one in which the background color doesn't show up — it's replaced by the background color that's visible in the browser. Consider making your images transparent if the background is likely to be a distraction or if the important part of your image is not rectangular. Take a look at the following figure, which shows an image with a regular background (at top) and the same image with a transparent background (bottom).

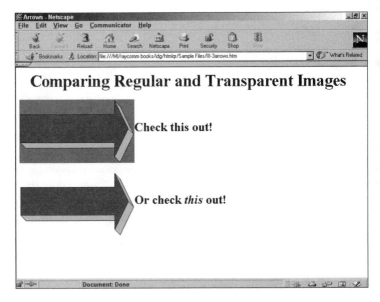

If you want to use transparent backgrounds, you must save them as GIF images, Version *89a*. You should have selections in your Save As dialog box that let you select both GIF and the specific version number — Version 87a or 89a — as you're saving your GIF image. JPG images *cannot* be transparent.

Many graphics or photo-editing software packages allow you to easily make a background color transparent. If you don't have image-editing software and don't want to invest in it, you can check out freeware and shareware programs available on the Internet. Many of these programs offer menu options for choosing the background color (that is, the color that disappears in the browser).

To find freeware and shareware image-editing software, go to www.yahoo.com/Computers_and_Internet/Software/ Graphics (capitalization counts!). Here, you find links to freeware and shareware programs and answers to Frequently Asked Questions.

To create transparent images, use a procedure similar to the following one. In these steps, we don't address the specifics for a particular software package; instead, we give you the general process for using any package.

*Note:* Before beginning, be sure that you have your image-editing software open and ready to use.

Follow these steps:

*1.* Open an image in your graphics software program.

*Note:* The image must have a uniform background color.

*2.* Locate your options for selecting a background color.

Many programs have a Background Color option under one of the menus, but this option varies greatly from program to program. (In Paint Shop Pro, for example, select the dropper tool, and then right-click the background color.)

*3.* Select the existing background color (the one you want to be transparent).

*4.* Go to the Save As dialog box, and type a name and a location.

(Make sure that you save the image as a GIF 89a image!)

*5.* Look for Save As options (probably accessible by clicking an Options button), and select an option that specifies "Make Background Color Transparent" or something similar.

*6.* Click OK (to get out of the Options dialog box), and then click Save to — well — save the image.

At this point, you don't see a change in the image background; you must open the image in your browser to see the results of your hard work. In any case, you should go ahead and view the image in your browser just to make sure that the image looks how you want it to look. In your browser, choose File⇨Open or File⇨Open Page, select Show All Files at the bottom of the dialog box that appears, find the image file you want to view, and then click Open.

## *Addressing Image Download Speed*

Images take quite a while to download (particularly over a slow Internet connection), and your readers are likely to give up on your Web site and move on if the images take too long to appear on-screen. (By the way, this situation is why the Web is often called the "World Wide Wait.") If you're on a fast Internet connection or if you're testing your HTML documents directly from your hard drive (as most of us do), you probably don't notice how long some images take to load, but 28.8 or 56.6 Kbps modems (which are pretty common) take a long time to transfer images — sometimes up to several minutes.

Basically, you can shorten the "World Wide Wait" in either of the following two ways:

✔ You can reduce the image file size.

✔ You can indicate image dimensions in the HTML document.

Thumbnail images, covered in Part IV, can also be helpful in managing the "World Wide Wait" when you want to use large images.

## Reducing file size

One of the best ways you can help speed image download time is to reduce the image file size. The following techniques can help reduce image file size and make an incredible difference in how fast they load:

✔ **Reduce color depth.** Check your image-editing software for options such as Reduce Color Depth. For fairly simple graphics, reducing the color depth to 16 colors, instead of 256 colors or millions of colors, can make the image's file size much smaller with little or no visible difference in the image quality.

✔ **Use the JPG or PNG formats for photographs.** Remember that these formats compress photographs and complex images more effectively than the GIF format does. Additionally, programs that allow you to save by using these formats also usually offer a place to set compression options. Experiment with the compression and increase compression until you start to see a loss of quality; then back off a little.

Because JPG compression is lossy — meaning that some of the data comprising the photograph is actually discarded during compression — try to avoid recompressing already compressed images. If you compress, recompress, and then recompress again, you may end up with artifacts, which are funny markings within the image. Better to compress only one time with the correct compression ratio — that is, try a compression of, say, 10. If needed, undo the compression or revert to the original image and then try 20.

✔ **Use the** LOWSRC="..." **attribute in the image tag in addition to the regular** SRC="..." **attribute.** ( The code would look something like <IMG SRC="regular.gif" LOWSRC= "verycompressed.jpg" >.) The LOWSRC= attribute points to a very highly compressed JPG file (that is, a very small one) that has the same dimensions as the image pointed to by SRC=. The very small image loads first and gives readers something to look at while the larger (main) image loads. This nonstandard attribute works only in Netscape Navigator but does not cause any problems on other browsers, so it may be worth trying.

## Specifying image size

You can improve how fast images seem to load by specifying the dimensions of the image in the HTML code. In doing so, browsers leave space for the image, finish loading the text (at which point your readers can start reading), and then continue loading the images. The images don't actually load faster, but specifying image size can help readers think they're loading faster, which is almost as good.

You specify the dimensions of the image (generally displayed in the title bar or status bar of image-editing programs) by including height and width attributes in the <IMG> tag. The numbers you specify for height and width specify the size in *pixels*, which are those itty-bitty dots on-screen that make up the image. (If you look really close at your screen, you can actually see the little pixels — aren't they tiny?!)

The following table shows the attributes used to specify image height and width.

| HTML Attribute | Effect | Use in Pairs? |
|---|---|---|
| HEIGHT=n | Specifies the height of the image in pixels. | No |
| WIDTH=n | Specifies the width of the image in pixels. | No |

The following example shows you how to include image dimensions in an <IMG> tag.

*Note:* Before beginning, make sure that you have your browser and text editor open with an HTML document loaded. You should have an image in the document as well.

To include the dimensions of the image in an <IMG> tag, follow these steps:

**1.** Open the image in your image-editing software, and find the dimensions.

These dimensions probably appear in the title bar at the top of the window or in the status bar at the bottom of the window. They're generally given as horizontal and then vertical.

**2.** Add the WIDTH= and HEIGHT= attributes, as follows:

```
<!DOCTYPE HTML PUBLIC "-//W3C//DTD HTML 4.01
    Frameset//EN"
    "http://www.w3.org/TR/html4/frameset.dtd">
<HTML>
<HEAD><TITLE>Lucy Looks</TITLE></HEAD>
<BODY>
<H1>Look, Lucy, Look!</H1>
```

```
<P><IMG SRC="lucy2a.gif" ALT="Lucy Looking
   Right" WIDTH=200 HEIGHT=157>
Lucy liked checking out interesting stuff when
   she was a kitten.</P>
</BODY>
</HTML>
```

You haven't really changed anything's appearance; these attributes just help the page appear to load more quickly by telling the browser what size image to expect.

## Controlling Image Alignment

Just as you can control how big or small an image is, you can also control how the images align with other elements on the page. By default, browsers align images on the left side of the page. If you want, you can realign them so that the images appear aligned at the right or aligned vertically, as you want. (If you're going to use alignment attributes, make sure that your readers don't use completely antiquated browsers, which don't support these attributes.)

 HTML 4.0 (and 4.01) recommends that you use style sheets to control image alignment, rather than using the attributes given here. Unless most of your readers will be using browsers that support style sheets (such as Microsoft Internet Explorer 4.0, which fully supports style sheets, or Netscape Navigator 4.0, which mostly supports style sheets, or later browsers), you must continue using these attributes. *See also* Part X for more about style sheets.

The following table shows the attributes used to control image alignment.

| HTML Attribute | Effect | Use in Pairs? |
|---|---|---|
| ALIGN="bottom" | Aligns the bottom of the image with the baseline of the current line. | No |
| ALIGN="left" | Allows an image to float down and over to the left margin (into the next available space); subsequent text wraps to the right of that image. | No |
| ALIGN="middle" | Aligns the baseline of the current line with the middle of the image. | No |
| ALIGN="right" | Aligns the image with the right margin and wraps the text around the left. | No |
| ALIGN="top" | Aligns the text with the top of the tallest item in the line. | No |

| HTML Attribute | Effect | Use in Pairs? |
|---|---|---|
| HSPACE=n | Controls the horizontal space (white space) around the image in pixels. | No |
| VSPACE=n | Controls the vertical space (white space) around the image in pixels. | No |

All you need to do is include these attributes in the <IMG> tag in your HTML document. The order of the attributes within the <IMG> tag isn't important. You can put them in the order that you find most convenient. The following sections show you how to use the various alignment options.

## Changing alignment

The following example shows you how to change image alignment.

*Note:* Before beginning, make sure that you have your browser and text editor open and ready to create a new document. Or you can apply this information to an existing document. You should have an image available to include in this document.

To change the alignment of your image in relation to the surrounding text, follow these steps:

*1.* Start your HTML document.

We started with a basic HTML document similar to the following example:

```
<!DOCTYPE HTML PUBLIC "-//W3C//DTD HTML 4.01
    Frameset//EN"
    "http://www.w3.org/TR/html4/frameset.dtd">
<HTML>
<HEAD><TITLE>Lucy Looks</TITLE></HEAD>
<BODY>
<H1>Look, Lucy, Look!</H1>
<P>Lucy liked checking out interesting stuff
when she was a kitten. Actually, she was
pretty much a pain. Not only did she look at
everything, she got into everything. We were
just discussing the number of times she
climbed up the screen door, only to get
stuck at the very top. Of course, now she's
a fatso and would tear the door down if she
even tried to climb up it. What's more, now
that she's grown, she's also afraid of her
own shadow. After she leaked outside the
other day, she spent the next 30 minutes
yowling and slinking around the house as if
```

```
the beetles were after her.</P>
</BODY>
</HTML>
```

*Note:* The term "leaked" in these examples describes the way
cats move into or out of the house — in whichever direction
they're not supposed to go. It's a bit technical, but we thought
that using the correct term was preferable to "sneaked" outside. (For all you who wondered whose flower bed was
violated, shame on you!)

2. Add the <IMG> tag along with the SRC and ALT attributes, as
   follows:

```
<H1>Look, Lucy, Look!</H1>
<P><IMG SRC="lucy.jpg" ALT="Lucy Looking
   Right">
Lucy liked checking out interesting stuff when
     she was a kitten. Actually, she was pretty
     much a pain. Not only did she look at. . .
```

The following figure shows the result of this initial alignment of
image and text.

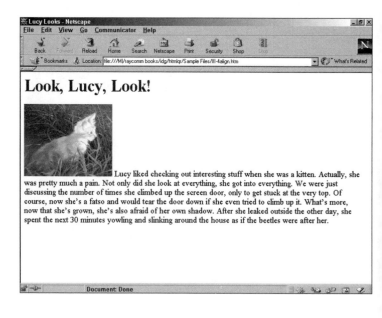

*3.* Add the ALIGN attribute, as shown in the following example.

Start by using ALIGN="LEFT". (This attribute allows your text to wrap around to the right of the image.) The next figure shows the result of this change in alignment between text and image.

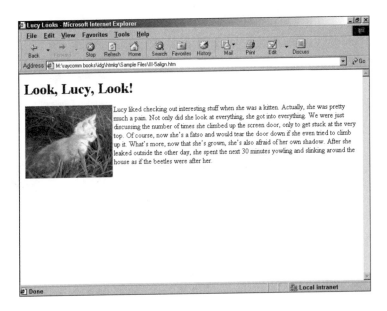

```
<P><IMG SRC="lucy.jpg" ALT="Lucy Looking Right"
    ALIGN="LEFT">
```

## Using multiple alignment options

If you insert several of the tags at once, you can see the differences in the effects. This example includes images with ALIGN="bottom", and ALIGN="middle".

*Note:* This example builds on the same basic document used in the previous example.

```
<H1>
<IMG SRC="lucysm.jpg" ALT="Lucy Looking Right"
ALIGN="bottom">Look, Lucy, Look!
<IMG SRC="lucysm.jpg" ALT="Lucy Looking Right"
ALIGN="middle">
<P>Lucy liked checking out interesting stuff when
she was a kitten. Actually, she was pretty. . .
```

The following figure shows the results of each type of alignment.

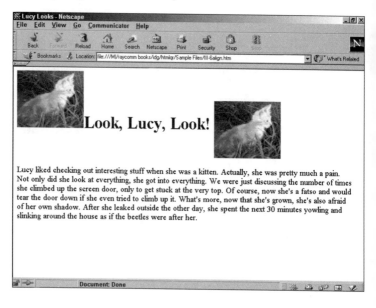

Experiment with the alignment tags until you find the most effective ones for your particular case.

In previous editions of this book, we included an example of bottom, middle, and top alignment. However, in the most common browsers, "top" now aligns with the tallest object on the line (the image itself) rather than the top of the tallest character, so if you have three images with bottom, middle, and top alignment, it looks just like bottom, middle, and bottom. Weirdness.

## Using alignment to create interesting effects

You can also insert several images by using complementary ALIGN attributes to produce interesting layout effects. (Unfortunately, you have no way to flip images in HTML; we used an image-editing program to make a mirror image of the first one.) The following example shows how to add a second image with right alignment to complement the existing image.

*Note:* This example builds on the same basic document that the previous example used.

```
<H1>Look, Lucy, Look!</H1>
<IMG SRC="lucy.jpg" ALT="Lucy Looking Right"
ALIGN="left">
<IMG SRC="lucyl.jpg" ALT="Lucy Looking Left"
ALIGN="right">
<P>Lucy liked checking out interesting stuff when
she was a kitten. Actually, she was pretty. . .
```

The following figure shows the results of these alignment options.

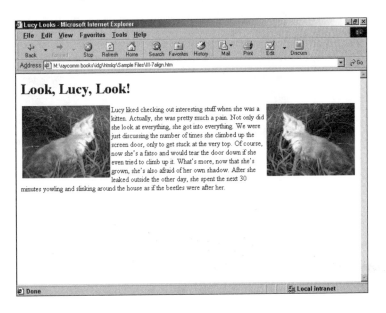

## Using horizontal and vertical spacing

You can include these alignment effects by adding vertical and horizontal space around the images.

Just add the HSPACE=n or VSPACE=n attributes (or both). The n is the number of pixels wide that the space should be on each side of the image; thus, the total width added is two times n.

*Note:* This example builds on the previous one by adding extra horizontal space around the existing images.

```
<H1>Look, Lucy, Look!</H1>
<P>
<IMG SRC="lucy.jpg" ALT="Lucy Looking Right"
ALIGN="left" HSPACE=40>
<IMG SRC="lucy1.jpg" ALT="Lucy Looking Left"
ALIGN="right" HSPACE=40>
<P>Lucy liked checking out interesting stuff when
she was a kitten. Actually, she was pretty. . .
```

The following figure shows the results of the extra space around the images.

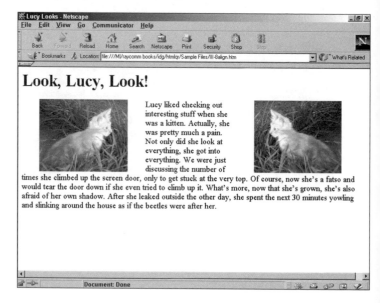

*Note:* If most of your readers will be using HTML 4.0-compliant browsers, consider achieving the same effects with style sheets, covered in Part VIII.

# Using Images for Linking

Back in Part III, we showed you how to include images in your HTML documents, as well as provided tips and ideas for making images efficient and part of your overall Web page design. In this part, we focus on using images as links and creating imagemaps (those cool clickable images).

In this part, we assume that you are already familiar with the `<IMG>` tag and its attributes, as well as with those tips and ideas on how to make images efficient and effective, as they apply to image links and imagemaps, too. You might review Part III before getting started with this part, if you need a refresher on these topics.

**See also** Part I before beginning this part if you need a quick recap of basic tags. Most of the examples in this part include only the tags and attributes discussed in this part and do not include structure or body tags.

## In this part . . .

Making Images into Links . . . . . . . . . . . . . . . . . . . . . 68
Creating Clickable Images . . . . . . . . . . . . . . . . . . . . 74

## Making Images into Links

You can use images as your anchors for making links. Using images as anchors isn't any more complicated than creating a link and then adding an image.

The following example shows you how to use an image as an anchor to link to another document.

*Note:* Before beginning, make sure that you have your browser and text editor open and ready to create a new document. Or you can apply this information to an existing document. You should have an image available to use in your document and another document available to which to link.

To use an image as the anchor to link to another document, follow these steps:

*1.* Start your HTML document.

Your document may look similar to the following example:

```
<!DOCTYPE HTML PUBLIC "-//W3C//DTD HTML 4.01
    Frameset//EN"
    "http://www.w3.org/TR/html4/frameset.dtd">
<HTML>
<HEAD><TITLE>Cat Gallery</TITLE></HEAD>
<BODY>
<H1>Cats in Our Lives (for Better or
    Worse)</H1>
<P>We've got several cats that figure
    prominently in our lives, including:</P>
<UL>
<LI>Winchester
<LI>Lucy
<LI>Booker
</UL>
</BODY>
</HTML>
```

*2.* Add a link, as shown in the following example.

```
<P>
<UL>
<LI>Winchester
    <A HREF="winchbio.html">(Biography)</A>
<LI>Lucy
<LI>Booker
</UL>
```

*See also* Part II if you need a review on adding links.

3. Add the <IMG> tag where you want the image to appear, as follows:

```
<P>
<UL>
<LI>Winchester <A HREF="winchbio.html">
<IMG>(Biography)</A>
<LI>Lucy
<LI>Booker
</UL>
```

4. Add the SRC= attribute to the <IMG> tag, as follows.

(*Remember:* This attribute tells what graphic you're including in your HTML document.)

```
<P>
<UL>
<LI>Winchester <A HREF="winchbio.html">
    <IMG SRC="winchest.jpg">(Biography)</A>
<LI>Lucy
<LI>Booker
</UL>
```

5. Add the ALT= attribute to the <IMG> tag, as shown in the following example.

(*Remember:* This attribute tells what text to display if the image isn't displayed.)

```
<P>
<UL>
<LI>Winchester <A HREF="winchbio.html">
<IMG SRC="winchest.jpg" ALT="Link to
  Winchester's Biography">(Biography)</A>
<LI>Lucy
<LI>Booker
</UL>
```

The Web page looks something like the following figure.

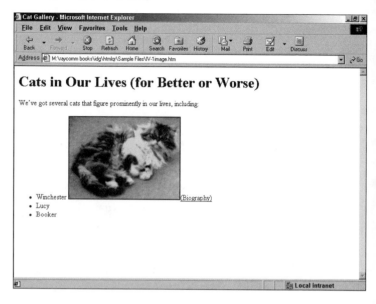

Notice that the image in this example has a border around it. The border is the same color as other links in the document, which indicates to your readers that the image links to other information or files.

## Using thumbnails

*Thumbnail* images are very small copies of bigger images that are linked to those bigger images. Readers seeing a page full of thumbnail images get the idea of what the pictures look like but don't need to wait all day for the bigger images to download.

We'd particularly recommend using thumbnails if you have many images or very large images in a page or if the images really stand alone and aren't necessary to support the surrounding text. Using thumbnails in this way isn't any more complicated than making a link and adding an image.

The following example shows you how to use a thumbnail to link to a larger image.

*Note:* Before beginning, make sure that you have your browser and text editor open and ready to create a new document. Or you can apply this information to an existing document. You should have an image available to link into your document and another document available to which to link. You also need to have ready a thumbnail-sized image — about 100 x 100 pixels or less — which you link to your full-sized image. (*See* "Specifying image size," in Part III, for more information about pixels.)

To link a thumbnail image to a larger image, follow these steps:

*1.* Start your HTML document.

The document should look something like the following example:

```
<!DOCTYPE HTML PUBLIC "-//W3C//DTD HTML 4.01
    Frameset//EN"
    "http://www.w3.org/TR/html4/frameset.dtd">
<HTML>
<HEAD><TITLE>Cat Gallery</TITLE></HEAD>
<BODY>
<H1>Cats in Our Lives (for Better or
    Worse)</H1>
<P>We've got several cats that figure
    prominently in our lives, including:</P>
<UL>
<LI>Winchester
<LI>Lucy
<LI>Booker
</UL>
</BODY>
</HTML>
```

*2.* Add an <IMG> tag, complete with SRC= and ALT= attributes, as follows.

(This attribute should point to the thumbnail — the smaller image.)

```
<UL>
<LI>Winchester <IMG SRC="winthumb.jpg"
    ALT="Winchester Thumbnail">
<LI>Lucy
<LI>Booker
</UL>
```

*3.* Add anchor tags around the image, as follows:

```
<UL>
<LI>Winchester <A><IMG SRC="winthumb.jpg"
    ALT="Winchester Thumbnail"></A>
<LI>Lucy
<LI>Booker
</UL>
```

**4.** Add the HREF= attribute, as the following example shows.

This attribute should point to the larger image.

```
<UL>
<LI>Winchester <A HREF="winbig.jpg"><IMG
    SRC="winthumb.jpg" ALT="Winchester
    Thumbnail"></A>
<LI>Lucy
<LI>Booker
</UL>
```

Your result looks somewhat like the following figure.

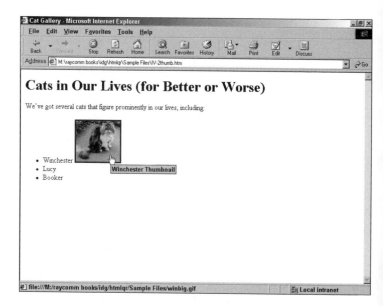

Notice that the image in this example has a border around it. The border is the same color as the color of other links in the document. This border tells your readers that the image links to something. (*Note:* We increased the border size by using the instructions from the following section so that the border would be clear in this illustration.)

In this example, we chose to use a very small, highly compressed (and, therefore, low-quality) JPG format image as the thumbnail so that the page loads quickly. The thumbnail links to a much larger and higher-quality image. We assume that if people like Winchester's picture enough to try to view the larger one, they don't mind waiting for a big image to load.

You can choose not to have the colored border appear around the thumbnail (or around all other images used as anchors). Just add the BORDER= attribute to the <IMG> tag with a value of BORDER=0, as shown in the following example.

*Note:* This example builds on the previous one.

```
<UL>
<LI>Winchester <A HREF="winbig.jpg"><IMG
    SRC="winthumb.jpg" ALT="Winchester Thumbnail"
    BORDER=0></A>
<LI>Lucy
<LI>Booker
</UL>
```

The following figure shows the same thumbnail without the border.

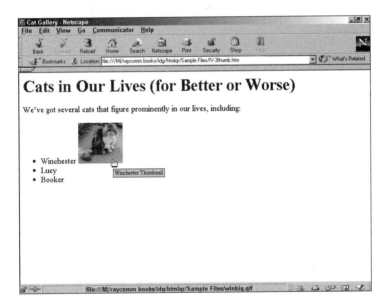

If you remove the border, your readers don't necessarily know that the image is a link because no visual cues indicate that they are to click the image. Removing a border is a neat trick, but it's not always a good idea.

If you don't want the border around the image, you can add the BORDER=0 attribute to the <IMG> tag. Without any visual cues, however, your readers probably won't know that the image is a link. Just make sure that your intent is clearly communicated to your readers.

You don't need to leave the text in the anchor (<u>Biography</u>, in this example) if you don't want to. Telling your readers what they're linking to, however, is a good idea. You can also, of course, give them this information by providing cues, such as text, in the link itself or in the rest of the page.

## Creating Clickable Images

You can use *clickable images* (also called *imagemaps*) to let readers click images or parts of images to link to other pages or images. The imagemap can provide a menu of selections for your reader, just as a set of regular links can provide a menu.

Imagemaps are good for making spiffy-looking menus — that is, so that readers can click various parts of an image to link to different information. Imagemaps are also good for making geographic-related links (by letting people click the state or country of their choice) or for all kinds of orientation or training applications (by allowing people to click to get more information about whatever is pictured).

The map controls are run either by browser or server software. Browser software controls *client-side imagemaps*. Server software controls older, less efficient, *server-side imagemaps*.

The main difference between client-side and server-side imagemaps is that client-side are more efficient and server-side require some help from your system administrator. Because we thrive on efficiency and can't guess how your system administrator has set up server-side imagemaps, we cover only client-side imagemaps in this book. Check with your system administrator for the server-side specifics.

If you decide to provide either kind of imagemap in your HTML document, particularly client-side imagemaps, you should also include an alternative means of navigating your documents (such as text links or buttons). Remember that not all your readers can or choose to use the imagemaps, so they need text links or buttons to navigate.

Keep in mind that some people choose not to (or cannot) view images, so imagemaps alone won't always work for navigation. Be sure to include text-based links to supplement your imagemap.

Including imagemaps in your HTML document is fairly easy. The processes for including client-side and server-side imagemaps are very similar. Just follow these steps:

*1.* Add an image to your HTML document.

*2.* Define clickable areas (a process called *mapping*).

*3.* Define the map — that is, specify which imagemap areas link to what information.

The following table shows the tags used to add an imagemap to an HTML document.

| HTML Tag or Attribute | Effect | Use in Pairs? |
|---|---|---|
| `<IMG SRC="...">` | Inserts an image. | No |
| *ISMAP* | Specifies that the image is a server-side clickable imagemap. | No |
| `USEMAP="#mapname"` | Identifies the picture as a client-side imagemap and specifies a MAP to use for acting on the readers' clicks. | No |

The `SRC="..."` attribute still points to a valid URL (relative or absolute) for your image. The remaining information points to an addition to the HTML document. Remember that all the other valid `<IMG>` attributes also apply to your imagemap.

## Adding the image

The image you find or create to use in the imagemap should be as clear and small as you can make it. Stick to a few colors and think simple. Although your readers may be impressed with a graphical masterpiece the first time they see it, they quickly tire of waiting for it to load each time they view your page.

We created the following simple image to illustrate some of the possibilities of imagemaps.

This example shows you how to include the image in your HTML document.

*Note:* Before beginning, make sure that you have your browser and text editor open with an HTML document loaded. You should have an image ready to use as well. We start with the following HTML document:

```
<!DOCTYPE HTML PUBLIC "-//W3C//DTD HTML 4.01
    Frameset//EN"
    "http://www.w3.org/TR/html4/frameset.dtd">
<HTML>
<HEAD>
<TITLE>Making Imagemaps</TITLE>
</HEAD>
<BODY>
<H1>Making Imagemaps Can Be Fun!</H1>
The image above is an imagemap.<P>
</BODY>
</HTML>
```

To include the image in your HTML document, follow these steps:

*1.* Include the image in your document, along with the appropriate ALT= information, by adding the following tags and text to the document:

```
<H1>Making Imagemaps Can Be Fun!</H1>
<IMG ALT="This is a clickable map."
    SRC="imagemap.jpg">
The image above is an imagemap.<P>
```

*2.* Include the USEMAP= attribute to indicate that the image is to be a client-side imagemap.

The USEMAP= attribute points to a map by name — we use the name demomap for this example, as follows:

```
<H1>Making Imagemaps Can Be Fun!</H1>
<IMG ALT="This is a clickable map."
    SRC="imagemap.jpg" USEMAP="#demomap">
The image above is an imagemap.<P>
```

*Note:* The # before demomap indicates that you're using a map within the same document, just as the # in a <A> tag indicates a within-document link.

You just added the image into your document and indicated that it's an imagemap. You can't see much of a difference through your browser — the image looks like any other image that's a link in your document. You must define the map before the hot spots work. Read on.

## Mapping clickable areas

In mapping clickable areas, you divide the image into parts that eventually link to other information and pages. Mapping is sort of like taking a picture and carving it into individual pieces (like puzzle pieces) — each piece represents an individual area that you can then link to something else.

Mapping your image isn't too complicated at all. All points or coordinates are measured from the upper-left corner of the image, in $x, y$ coordinates. That point on the image is 0,0 — zero pixels across by zero pixels down. The following image shows the cursor pointing at (focused on?) that spot. Notice that you can see the coordinates (0,0) at the lower left of the window.

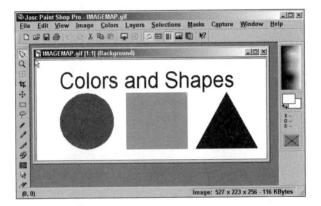

**See also** the section "Specifying image size," in Part III, for more information about pixels.

This example identifies the coordinates for each of the three shapes in our sample image. These three shapes show you all you need to know to map all shapes. By identifying the coordinates of certain points in a figure, as described in the following list, you can describe any shape:

- ✓ Rectangular shapes require the upper-left and lower-right corners. The computer figures out the rest.

- ✓ Circles require the center and the radius length. (Yes, you must do the math to figure out the radius.)

- ✓ Polygons, such as our triangle, just require each corner. The computer connects the dots to finish the figure.

You can represent any other shape by using some combination of the rectangle, circle, and polygon. A sleeping cat, for example, can have a long rectangle for the tail, a fatter one for the body, a circle for the head, and a couple of triangles for the ears. Alternatively, you can just go point to point to point on the cat and call it a fancy polygon.

You need to be close on the coordinates, but they don't have to be exact. If you find yourself straining to get the cursor right on the precise point (as we did to get the 0,0 coordinate), you're working too hard. Your readers are just going to point at the image and click — probably not aiming for the very edge. And if you're trying to map lots of shapes or make a clickable map of your city, you should probably check out one of the mapping programs available on the Internet to ease the process. Go to your favorite searching site, such as Yahoo! (www.yahoo.com) or AltaVista (www.altavista.com) and type and look for **imagemap**. We recommend Mapedit or Liveimage for Windows, Gimp for UNIX/Linux and Webmap for Macintosh.

## Mapping a rectangle

This section shows how to determine the coordinates for rectangles used in imagemaps.

*Note:* Before beginning, you should have a sample image open in an image-editing program and a pencil and paper to note the coordinates.

To determine the coordinates that define a rectangle, follow these steps:

*1.* Point the cursor at the upper-left corner of the rectangle, and write the *x,y* coordinates (208,75), as shown in the following figure.

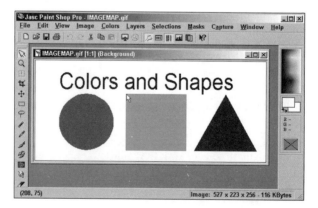

*2.* Point at the lower-right corner and write the *x,y* coordinates (345,197), as the following figure shows.

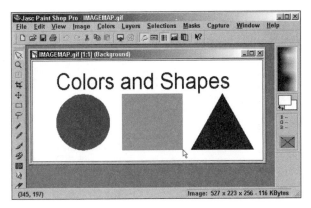

## Mapping a circle

This section shows how to determine the coordinates for circles used in imagemaps.

*Note:* Make sure that you have your sample image open in an image-editing program.

To determine the coordinates of a circle, follow these steps:

*1.* Point the cursor at the center of the circle, as shown in the following figure, and write the coordinates (118,133, in this example).

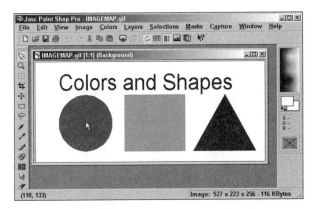

*2.* Move the cursor horizontally to the edge of the circle, as the following figure shows, and note those coordinates, too (178,133, in this example).

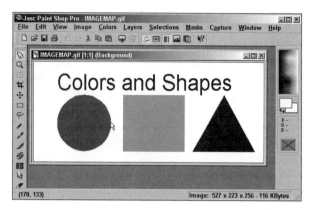

3. Subtract the first *x* coordinate from the second one.

   In our example, we subtract 118 from 178 and get 60. That's the radius of the circle.

## Mapping a polygon

This section shows how to determine the coordinates for other shapes used in imagemaps.

*Note:* Make sure that you have your sample image open in an image-editing program.

To determine the coordinates that define the triangle (or any other polygon), follow these steps:

1. Pick a corner, point the cursor at it, as shown in the following figure, and note the *x,y* coordinates.

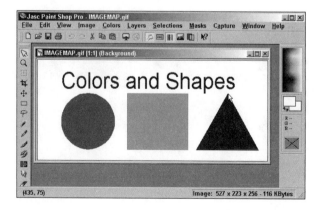

2. Move to the next corner, as the following figure shows, and note those coordinates.

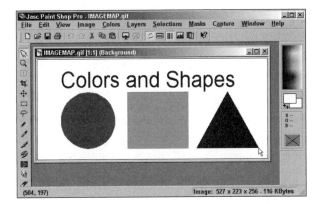

Continue moving around the edge of the shape, noting the coordinates of each corner. Make sure that you mark the corners in order — the computer connects the dots in the same order that you follow to figure out what the shape is.

Don't lose the piece of paper with your notes. You need it to define your map.

## Defining the map

Defining the map simply tells the computer which areas readers may click and what link to follow after they click. The process looks more complex than it really is. The following table shows the tags and attributes used to define the map.

| HTML Tag or Attribute | Effect | Use in Pairs? |
|---|---|---|
| `<MAP>...`<br>`</MAP>` | Specifies a collection of hot spots for a client-side imagemap. | Yes |
| `NAME="..."` | Gives the MAP a name so that it can be referred to later. | No |
| `<AREA>` | Specifies the shape of a hot spot in a client-side imagemap. | No |
| `COORDS="x1,y1,`<br>`x2,y2, ..."` | Specifies coordinates that define the hot spot's shape. | No |
| `HREF="URL"` | Specifies the destination of the hot spot. | No |

**cont.**

| HTML Tag or Attribute | Effect | Use in Pairs? |
|---|---|---|
| *NOHREF* | Indicates that clicks in this region should cause no action. | No |
| *SHAPE="..."* | Specifies type of shape as RECT (for rectangle), CIRC (for circle), or POLY (for polygon). | No |

The <MAP>...</MAP> tag tells the browser which areas in your image link to which URLs. This example shows you how to include a map definition in your document along with the imagemap.

*Note:* Before beginning, make sure that you have your browser and text editor open with an HTML document loaded. You should have an image in the document as well. We continue here with the previous example:

```
<!DOCTYPE HTML PUBLIC "-//W3C//DTD HTML 4.01
    Frameset//EN"
    "http://www.w3.org/TR/html4/frameset.dtd">
<HTML>
<HEAD>
<TITLE>Making Imagemaps</TITLE>
</HEAD>
<BODY>
<H1>Making Imagemaps Can Be Fun!</H1>
<IMG ALT="This is a clickable map."
    SRC="imagemap.jpg" USEMAP="#demomap"><P>
The image above is an imagemap.<P>
</BODY>
</HTML>
```

To include a map definition in your document along with the imagemap, follow these steps:

*1.* Include the <MAP> tags in your document, as shown in the following example:

```
<IMG ALT="This is a clickable map."
    SRC="imagemap.jpg" USEMAP="#demomap"><P>
The image above is an imagemap.<P>
<MAP>
</MAP>
</BODY>
</HTML>
```

2. Add the NAME= attribute to the <MAP> tag, as the following example shows.

   *Note:* Our example calls the map demomap.

   ```
   <IMG ALT="This is a clickable map."
       SRC="imagemap.jpg" USEMAP="#demomap"><P>
   The image above is an imagemap.<P>
   <MAP NAME="demomap">
   </MAP>
   </BODY>
   </HTML>
   ```

3. Add an <AREA> tag between the <MAP> tags, as follows.

   You eventually have one <AREA> tag for each clickable area in your map, but we build them one at a time.

   ```
   <IMG ALT="This is a clickable map."
       SRC="imagemap.jpg" USEMAP="#demomap"><P>
   The image above is an imagemap.<P>
   <MAP NAME="demomap">
   <AREA>
   </MAP>
   ```

4. Add a SHAPE= attribute to the <AREA> tag, as follows.

   We're starting with SHAPE="RECT" because the square (rectangle) is the easiest one to do.

   ```
   <IMG ALT="This is a clickable map."
       SRC="imagemap.jpg" USEMAP="#demomap"><P>
   The image above is an imagemap.<P>
   <MAP NAME="demomap">
   <AREA SHAPE="RECT">
   </MAP>
   ```

5. Add the COORDS= attribute to the <AREA> tag, as shown in the following example.

   The coordinates for our square are 208,75 for the upper-left corner and 345,197 for the lower-right corner.

   ```
   <IMG ALT="This is a clickable map."
       SRC="imagemap.jpg" USEMAP="#demomap"><P>
   The image above is an imagemap.<P>
   <MAP NAME="demomap">
   <AREA SHAPE="RECT" COORDS="208,75,345,197">
   </MAP>
   ```

   *Note:* Do not include spaces between the coordinates.

**6.** Add the HREF= attribute to the <AREA> tag, as follows.

You can use any valid URL for your client-side imagemap.

```
<IMG ALT="This is a clickable map."
    SRC="imagemap.jpg" USEMAP="#demomap"><P>
The image above is an imagemap.<P>
<MAP NAME="demomap">
<AREA SHAPE="RECT" COORDS="208,75,345,197"
    HREF="/shapes/square.htm">
</MAP>
```

**7.** Add more <AREA> tags as necessary.

Make sure that you include the correct SHAPE= and COORDS= attributes for each tag. The following example includes the coordinates we noted or calculated in the section "Mapping clickable areas," earlier in this part.

```
<IMG ALT="This is a clickable map."
    SRC="imagemap.jpg" USEMAP="#demomap"><P>
The image above is an imagemap.<P>
<MAP NAME="demomap">
<AREA SHAPE="RECT" COORDS="208,75,345,197"
    HREF="/shapes/square.htm">
<AREA SHAPE="CIRCLE" COORDS="118,133,60"
    HREF="/shapes/round.htm">
<AREA SHAPE="POLYGON"
    COORDS="435,75,504,197,363,196"
    HREF="/shapes/pointy.htm">
</MAP>
```

That's it! Now just load it in your browser, and try it out. The result should look something like the following figure.

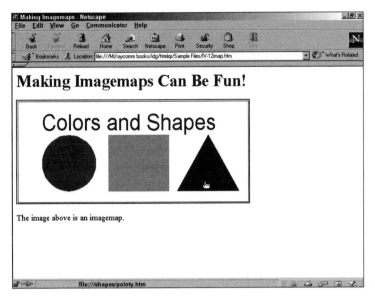

 You can overlap shapes if that helps you to set things up. The first shape that you define in the ⟨MAP⟩ tag is the one that takes precedence. As a matter of fact, a good idea may be to add one final rectangle that covers the entire area of the image with its own link for the people who click in the wrong place.

# Making Effective Web Pages

In this part, we introduce you to some really nifty things that you can do by using HTML. We also provide you with guidelines on how to use them effectively.

You need to be pretty familiar with the basic tags before diving into this part. Most of the examples in this part include only the tags and attributes discussed under a particular heading and do not include structure or body tags. We assume that you know where structure and body tags go. If you don't, you may want to refer to Part I of this book.

## In this part . . .

Developing Tables . . . . . . . . . . . . . . . . . . . . . . . . . . . . 88

Embedding Horizontal Rules . . . . . . . . . . . . . . . . . . 91

Forcing Line Breaks . . . . . . . . . . . . . . . . . . . . . . . . . 93

Providing Author and Contact Information . . . . . . . 94

# *Developing Tables*

Tables — not just for dinner any more. In the context of HTML, tables are very handy for the following purposes:

🖛 Lining up material vertically and horizontally

🖛 Making creative layouts

🖛 Placing text next to graphics

The following table shows the tags and attributes used to create tables.

| HTML Tag or Attribute | Effect | Use in Pairs? |
|---|---|---|
| `<TABLE>... </TABLE>` | Indicates table format. | Yes |
| `BORDER=n` | Controls table border width in pixels. 0 specifies no border. | No |
| `<TD>...</TD>` | Indicates table data cell. | Yes |
| `<TH>...</TH>` | Indicates table headings. | Yes |
| `<TR>...</TR>` | Indicates table row items. | Yes |

The `<TD>`, `<TH>`, and `<TR>` tags do not have to be used in pairs according to the HTML 4.01 specification, but some older browsers work more reliably with tables if you use the closing tags. In the examples in this part, we use the closing tags for clarity.

This example shows you how to create a table with a couple of rows and columns.

*Note:* Before beginning, make sure that you have your browser and text editor open and ready to create a new document. Or you can apply this information to an existing document.

Our objective is to create a table containing the following information:

| Culprit | Water Balloon Skills |
|---|---|
| Deborah | Fair |
| Eric | Excellent |

To create a table with a couple of rows and a couple of columns, follow these steps.

1. Type your text, row by row, using a space or two between row elements, as follows:

```
Culprit Water Balloon Skills
Deborah Fair
Eric Excellent
```

2. Insert <TABLE> tags before and after the text to indicate the <TABLE> information that goes in the table, as shown here:

```
<TABLE>
Culprit Water Balloon Skills
Deborah Fair
Eric Excellent
</TABLE>
```

3. Add <TR> tags to show where the table rows go, as the following example shows.

   (*Remember:* Rows go across the page.)

```
<TABLE>
<TR>Culprit Water Balloon Skills</TR>
<TR>Deborah Fair</TR>
<TR>Eric Excellent</TR>
</TABLE>
```

4. Add pairs of <TH> tags to show where the table heading cells go (in the top row), as follows.

   At this point, adding some spacing may help you more easily see what's going on.

```
<TABLE>
<TR><TH>Culprit</TH>
<TH>Water Balloon Skills</TH>
</TR>
<TR>Deborah Fair</TR>
<TR>Eric Excellent</TR>
</TABLE>
```

5. Add pairs of <TD> tags to indicate the individual cells of a table, as shown here:

```
<TABLE>
<TR><TH>Culprit</TH>
<TH>Water Balloon Skills</TH>
</TR>
<TR><TD>Deborah</TD> <TD>Fair</TD></TR>
<TR><TD>Eric</TD> <TD>Excellent</TD></TR>
</TABLE>
```

**6.** Add the BORDER attribute to the <TABLE> tag to create lines around each table cell, as the following example shows:

```
<TABLE BORDER=1>
<TR><TH>Culprit</TH>
<TH>Water Balloon Skills</TH>
</TR>
<TR><TD>Deborah </TD> <TD>Fair</TD></TR>
<TR><TD>Eric </TD> <TD>Excellent</TD></TR>
</TABLE>
```

The following figure shows the results of all this work.

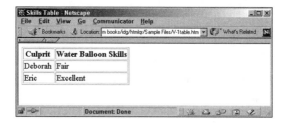

You can be creative with table borders if you want. You can, for example, create a table without borders — just don't include the BORDER=1 attribute in the <TABLE> tag. You should take this action if the table appears cluttered with many rows or columns o if you're using the table as a formatting tool (for example, if you want to include text next to a graphic). You can also increase the thickness of the border by increasing the number of the attribute BORDER=5, for example.

Experiment with tables. You can come up with many creative lay-outs and page designs. Here are some ideas:

✔ Embed images in tables (to align graphics and text the way yc want).

✔ Place text in table cells to make columns — like a newspaper.

✔ Place headings to the left (or right) of a paragraph of text.

If you find that your tables have problems — or don't seem to wo at all — make very sure that your tags are paired correctly and th you haven't omitted any tags. Printing the source and marking pairs of tags are sometimes necessary for troubleshooting tables. As you can see from the very small example in the text, getting co fused is easy with all the different tags necessary for tables. Additionally, save yourself some trouble by liberally using white space and blank lines as you create the table. The extra white space can help you see what's going on.

# Embedding Horizontal Rules

HTML allows you to break up Web pages by applying a horizontal rule, <HR>. This horizontal rule can serve not only as a visual break for long pages but also as an informational break. The following table illustrates the tag used to create horizontal rules and the attributes that let you format them.

Note that the HTML 4.01 standard recommends that you use style sheets to format your horizontal rules, rather than use the attributes listed here. *See* Part X and Appendix C for more information about style sheets.)

| HTML Tag or Attribute | Effect | Use in Pairs? |
|---|---|---|
| <HR> | Applies a horizontal rule. | No |
| SIZE="number" | Indicates how thick the rule is. | No |
| WIDTH="number" | Specifies an exact width in or percent (%) pixels or percent of document width. A percentage value must appear in quotes, like WIDTH="50%". | No |
| ALIGN="LEFT", CENTER, or RIGHT | Specifies the alignment; works only in combination with WIDTH. | No |

To use horizontal rules, apply the following tags and attributes.

*Note:* Before beginning, make sure that you have your browser and text editor open and ready to create a new document. Or you can apply this information to an existing document.

Follow these steps:

*1.* Start your HTML page; it should be something like the following:

```
<!DOCTYPE HTML PUBLIC "-//W3C//DTD HTML 4.01
    Frameset//EN"
    "http://www.w3.org/TR/html4/frameset.dtd">
    <HTML>
<HEAD><TITLE>Lost Cat!</TITLE></HEAD>
<BODY>
</BODY>
</HTML>
```

*2.* Enter the text between the <BODY> tags and put in a few horizontal rules, as shown in this example:

```
<P><EM><H1 ALIGN=CENTER>Lost
   Cat!</H1></EM></P>
<HR WIDTH=80% ALIGN=CENTER>
<HR WIDTH=60% ALIGN=CENTER>
<HR WIDTH=40% ALIGN=CENTER>
<P>Fuzzy tortoise shell Persian--lost in Big
   Lake area. Probably looks confused.</P>
<HR>
<P>Answers to:
<UL>
<LI>Winchester
<LI>Hairheimer
<LI>Fritter
<LI>Sound of can opener
</UL></P>
<P>Please call if you find him: 555-9999</P>
<HR WIDTH=200>
<HR WIDTH=400>
<HR WIDTH=200>
<P ALIGN=RIGHT><I>Thanks!</I></P>
```

The following figure shows the effects of these tags.

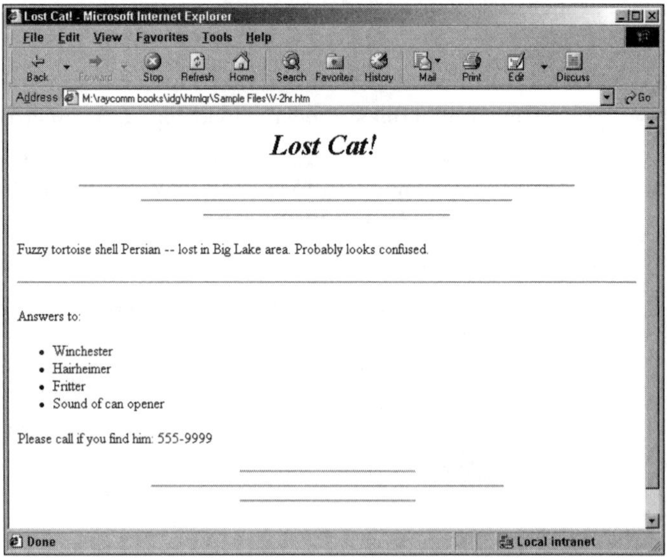

Getting carried away using horizontal rules, just as we did in this example, is not at all difficult. Our use of them here is definitely excessive. You should do as we say (not as we do) and use these rules only where they help readers find information more easily or help them wade through long passages of information.

Experiment with the SIZE, WIDTH, and ALIGN attributes. (The numbers used in the example are just that — examples of what you can do.) You can make the horizontal rules thinner, thicker, longer, or shorter, depending on the effect you want to achieve.

For your readers with HTML 4.0-compliant browsers, you can also use style sheets (covered in Part X) to format horizontal rules.

# Forcing Line Breaks

HTML allows you to break lines of text so that you can determine exactly (or as much as possible) how they appear on the users' end.

The following table shows the tag used to force line breaks.

| HTML Tag or Attribute | Effect | Use in Pairs? |
|---|---|---|
| <BR> | Breaks line; new line begins after tag. | No |
| CLEAR="..." | Requires that LEFT, RIGHT, NONE, or ALL margins are clear before new line starts. | No |

To break lines of text so that each line appears the way you want it to (for example, in a poem), use the <BR> tag.

*Note:* Before beginning, make sure that you have your browser and text editor open and ready to create a new document. Or you can apply this information to an existing document.

Follow these steps:

1. Start your HTML page, which should look something like the following example:

```
<!DOCTYPE HTML PUBLIC "-//W3C//DTD HTML 4.01
    Frameset//EN"
    "http://www.w3.org/TR/html4/frameset.dtd">
    <HTML>
<HEAD><TITLE>Ode to Food</TITLE></HEAD>
<BODY>
</BODY>
</HTML>
```

2. Type the information you want to include, with `<BR>` at the end of each line, as follows.

```
<BODY>
<P>
I'm Hungry, I'm Hungry! I said with a
    sigh,<BR>
I want to cancel dinner and go straight to my
    pie.<BR>
I want cake and ice cream and toast with
    jelly,<BR>
And I don't care if I grow a big belly.<BR>
</P>
</BODY>
```

If you are including a line break and want to make sure that the new line doesn't start until below an image, for example, you should add the `CLEAR=ALL` attribute to the `<BR>` tag. That forces the new line below all other objects on the line.

The following figure shows the effects of these line breaks.

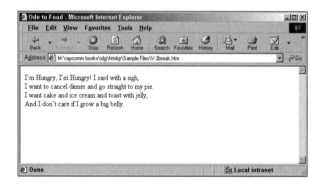

# Providing Author and Contact Information

Good Web pages provide information about the author or about how to contact the author. The first corollary to that statement is that good Web page authors (such as yourself) include their contact information in their pages. As a result, readers can follow up or obtain information not included on the Web site.

You can provide such information by doing one (or both) of two things:

✔ Use an address tag.

✔ Use a return e-mail hyperlink.

The following table shows a tag and a URL used to provide contact information.

| HTML Tag or URL | Effect | Use in Pairs? |
|---|---|---|
| MAILTO:yourid@your. email.address | Indicates a specific e-mail address for use in place of URLs in the HREF="..." attribute in an <A> tag. | No |
| <ADDRESS>... </ADDRESS> | Indicates address or contact information; generally appears in italics. | Yes |

## Using an address tag

Using an address is handy for indicating contact information. An address tag also helps users roaming the Internet seeking good Web pages to spot your address quickly. And as the Internet develops, it's likely that people will eventually be able to search for addresses (or any content within the <ADDRESS> tags).

*Note:* Before beginning, make sure that you have your browser and text editor open.

To use an address, just add the information near the bottom of your Web page, as shown in the following example.

```
<!DOCTYPE HTML PUBLIC "-//W3C//DTD HTML 4.01
   Frameset//EN"
   "http://www.w3.org/TR/html4/frameset.dtd">
<HTML>
<HEAD><TITLE>Winchester's Resume</TITLE></HEAD>
<BODY>
<H1 ALIGN=CENTER>Winchester's Resume</H1>
<P>
<UL>
<LI>I sleep.
<LI>I eat.
<LI>I cough up hairballs.
</UL>
</P>
<ADDRESS>Information provided by Deb and Eric
   Ray<BR>
(Winchester's Reluctant Owners)<BR>
Tulsa, OK 74114<BR>
(555) 222-1111<BR>
</ADDRESS>
</BODY>
</HTML>
```

The following figure shows the effects of this addition.

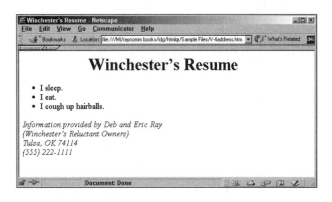

## Using an e-mail link

To provide really complete contact information, you can use an e-mail link that allows users to e-mail directly from the Web site.

To use an e-mail return, just add a link to the names in the identification section. Use the following URL (edited appropriately to show your real e-mail address):

```
mailto:your-email@your.address.com
```

**Note:** Before beginning, make sure that you have your browser and text editor open.

**See also** Part II if you read this section heading three times and still don't understand it.

```
<ADDRESS>Information provided by
<A HREF="mailto:authors→ycomm.com">Deb and Eric
   Ray</A><BR>
(Winchester's Reluctant Owners)<BR>
Tulsa, OK 74114<BR>
(555) 222-1111<BR>
</ADDRESS>
</BODY>
</HTML>
```

The following figure shows the new hyperlink in your document.

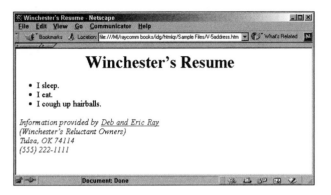

# Setting Background and Text Characteristics

In this part, we show you how to set background and text characteristics, which can help you liven up your pages with various color and alignment options. Note that some of the formatting attributes and tags in this part work with nearly all current browsers but are not recommended in HTML 4.0. If you know that your readers use HTML 4.0-compliant browsers, such as Microsoft Internet Explorer 4.0 (which is completely compliant) or Netscape Navigator 4.0 (which is mostly compliant), strongly consider using style sheets for all of your formatting needs. We show you throughout this part which formatting tricks are available using style sheets. *See also:* Part X of this book for the specifics on using style sheets.

As with Part V, you need to be pretty familiar with the basic tags before diving into this part. We assume that you know where structure and body tags go. If you don't, you may revisit Part I of this book.

## In this part . . .

Applying a Color Background . . . . . . . . . . . . . . . . 100

Applying an Image Background . . . . . . . . . . . . . . . 102

Setting Document Text Colors . . . . . . . . . . . . . . . 105

Specifying Text Alignment . . . . . . . . . . . . . . . . . 108

Using Type Specifications . . . . . . . . . . . . . . . . . . 110

# Applying a Color Background

To include a background color, all you need to do is insert the BGCOLOR= attribute in the opening <BODY> tag. (Or, you could follow the recommendations in the HTML 4.01 standard and use style sheets to accomplish the same thing, as covered in Part X.)

The following table shows the attribute used to specify background color in an HTML document.

| HTML Attribute | Effect | Use in Pairs? (for the <BODY> tag) |
|---|---|---|
| BGCOLOR= "#rrggbb" | Specifies the color name or number of the background. | No |

**Remember:** If your readers use the newest and coolest browsers — at least Microsoft Internet Explorer 4.0 or Netscape Navigator 4.0 or later — you could use style sheets, instead, for more control of backgrounds for both the whole documents and individual elements within the documents. **See also** Part X for more information about style sheets.

This example shows you how to add a background color.

**Note:** Before beginning the example in this section, make sure that you have your browser and text editor open and ready to create a new document. Or you can apply this information to an existing document.

To use a color background, follow these steps:

1. Start your HTML page.

   The page should look something like the following example:

   ```
   <!DOCTYPE HTML PUBLIC "-//W3C//DTD HTML 4.01
      Frameset//EN"
      "http://www.w3.org/TR/html4/frameset.dtd">
      <HTML>
   <HEAD><TITLE>Fleabag Kitty</TITLE></HEAD>
   <BODY>With a scratcha scratcha here and a
      scratcha scratcha there. . .
   </BODY>
   </HTML>
   ```

2. Add the BGCOLOR attribute to the <BODY> tag.

   For the following example, we use #3399CC (which is sky blue):

```
<HEAD><TITLE>Fleabag Kitty</TITLE></HEAD>
<BODY BGCOLOR="#3399CC">With a scratcha
    scratcha here and a scratcha scratcha there.
        . .
</BODY>
```

The following figure shows the results of this change.

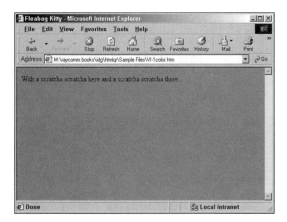

In the place of #RRGGBB, insert a hexadecimal number — just a combination of letters and numbers that means something to the computer but means something to you only with the help of a crib sheet (like the Cheat Sheet inside this book's front cover). To get a black background, for example, you use #000000. (If you specify a black background, look at the following section to specify colors for the text.)

***See also*** Part III for information about choosing hexadecimal RGB numbers appropriate for using in HTML documents. Especially because background colors span the entire page, you need to be sure you choose colors that will appear properly in readers' browsers.

Alternatively, you can specify some colors by name. The following colors work in most browsers: aqua, black, blue, fuchsia, gray, green, lime, maroon, navy, olive, purple, red, silver, teal, white, and yellow. The code would look something like BGCOLOR="purple".

***Remember:*** All text and graphics appear on top of the background; therefore, make sure that the color you choose is light enough so that the text remains easily readable.

## Finding RGB values

So just where do you come up with the RGB values? Try one of the
following five ways:

✓ **Use the Cheat Sheet at the front of this book.** Note that these
colors printed on the Cheat Sheet will vary slightly from what
you see on-screen (because of the differences in print and
online color representations); however, the Cheat Sheet gives
you a good starting point for choosing colors and finding RGB
values.

✓ **Find a background color that you like on an existing Web
page — and copy it!** Most, if not all, browsers provide a way for
you to view the HTML page used to create a Web site. Look for
the color number in the 〈BODY〉 tag for use in your own
documents.

Generally, if you're viewing a page from your browser, you can
choose View➪Page Source or View➪Source to see the HTML
codes used to create the document.

✓ **Check out Part III, the section called "Choosing colors carefully."** This section provides you with handy dandy information
about choosing RGB values and can help you choose ones that
look good in almost any browser.

✓ **Find a list of RGB numbers provided on the Web.** If you
browse enough on the Web, you're likely to find general sources
of information that provide you with lists of commonly used
Web page features, including RGB numbers, complete with samples.

✓ **Look for RGB values in your image-editing or paint software.**
Many of these packages offer you the option of altering the
colors with which you're working and provide you with the RGB
value for the colors that you choose. Look in the color-related
screens for RGB values.

# *Applying an Image Background*

In addition to using simple colors for backgrounds, you can use
images as backgrounds. The process is similar to adding a color,
except that you're adding an entire image. Again, here, you could
follow the recommendations in the HTML 4.01 standard and use
style sheets to accomplish the same thing, as covered in Part X.
The BACKGROUND attribute expects a URL (relative or absolute)
pointing to an image.

The background value is just a standard URL, so if the image is somewhere other than in the same folder as your document, you need to include the relative or absolute URL, not just the filename. The following table shows the attribute used to apply a background image to an HTML document.

| HTML Attribute (for <BODY> tag) | Effect | Use in Pairs? |
|---|---|---|
| BACKGROUND="..." | Places an image as a background. | No |

This example shows you how to use an image for the background of your HTML document.

*Note:* Before beginning, make sure that you have your browser and text editor open and ready to start a document. You can also apply this information to an existing document.

To use an image for a background, follow these steps:

*1.* Start your HTML page.

The page should look something like the following example:

```
<!DOCTYPE HTML PUBLIC "-//W3C//DTD HTML 4.01
   Frameset//EN"
   "http://www.w3.org/TR/html4/frameset.dtd">
<HTML>
<HEAD><TITLE>Fleabag Kitty</TITLE></HEAD>
<BODY>With a scratcha scratcha here and a
   scratcha scratcha there. . .</BODY>
</HTML>
```

*2.* Add the BACKGROUND="..." attribute, including an image filename, to the <BODY> tag, as follows:

```
<BODY BACKGROUND="flea.gif">With a scratcha
   scratcha here and a scratcha scratcha there.
   . .</BODY>
```

The following figure shows the flea.gif image (one flea) tiled throughout the page. Yes, it's really a flea, not a roach (ick!).

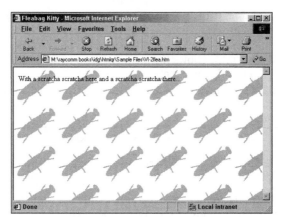

Background images, such as the flea.gif image, that do not fill the entire background are tiled to cover all the available space; that is, copies of the image are automatically placed together like a tile floor. The background image in the example is really only one flea — the copies are done automatically by the browser.

If you use a dark-colored image — and change the text colors to light hues so that they show up properly — make sure that you also change the background color to something dark. Otherwise, if the image doesn't load for some reason, the page will be unreadable.

## Finding images to use

Coming up with images to use for a background is about as easy as using simple colors. The only difference is that you use an image file rather than just a color number. Here are some ways to find background images:

✔ **Design your own.** You may want to use a background image that's specific to the Web site you're creating. We strongly suggest doing so if you have any graphics talent at all. (If you do what we do and make fleas that look like roaches, check out the other options.)

✔ **Find backgrounds that you like on the Web.** Don't just copy these and use them, but you can get good ideas on what looks good and what doesn't.

Keep in mind that copyright laws also apply to the Internet and that the ease of copying images doesn't equate to the appropriateness of doing so.

✔ **Look for image or background CDs or disks in your local software store.** Many CDs are available that have nothing but cool backgrounds.

Really good background images are *seamless*, meaning that they look just like one big image used as a background. The key is to make the edges match up evenly. Some image-editing software, such as the newest versions of Paint Shop Pro (check out www.jasc.com on the Web) can automatically make images seamless.

Make sure that you choose simple backgrounds — ones with no more than a few subtle colors or with only a few elements. Busy backgrounds make reading difficult for your users.

If you're one of those lucky people with a nice big monitor, high-quality video card, and really spiffy resolution, please take pity on the rest of us. Great background effects for you may be smudgy and unclear to many of us. Check out your effects on a low-end monitor.

If you like backgrounds that provide a vertical band down one side, you can create one by making very short (just a few pixels) and very wide (at least 1,280 pixels) images that look like a cross-section of the background effect you want. That image, after the browser tiles it, produces a band down the side of the monitor, as in the following figure.

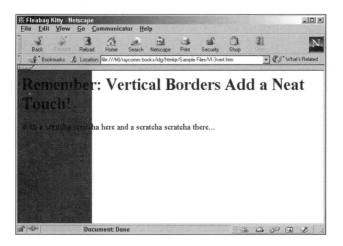

Style sheets, usable only in HTML 4.0-compliant browsers, let you control how background images are tiled — either horizontally, vertically, or both. *See also* Part X for more about style sheets.

# Setting Document Text Colors

In addition to changing the background of Web pages, you can also change the color of the text. This technique is particularly handy if you've used a background on which the default colors of text and links do not show up well.

Style sheets, usable only in HTML 4.0-compliant browsers, let you easily control document text colors as well. *See also* Part X for more about style sheets.

The following table shows the attributes used to color text in an HTML document.

| HTML Attribute | Effect | Use in Pairs? |
|---|---|---|
| TEXT="#RRGGBB" | Changes color of the body text. | No |
| LINK="#RRGGBB" | Changes color of the link. | No |
| ALINK="#RRGGBB" | Changes color of the active link. | No |
| VLINK="#RRGGBB" | Changes color of the visited link. | No |

You fill in a color number where "#RRGGBB" is indicated. In the following examples, we use BGCOLOR="#3399CC", TEXT="#FFFFFF", LINK="#FF0000", ALINK="#FFFF00", and VLINK="#8C1717". Because colors of text generally don't appear in a large mass, choosing one of the 216 "safe" color numbers is far less important for text.

## Changing text colors

This example shows you how to change text colors on your Web page.

*Note:* Before beginning, make sure that you have your browser and text editor open and ready to create a new document. Or you can apply this information to an existing document.

To change text colors on your Web page, follow these steps:

*1.* Start your HTML page.

The page should look similar to the following example:

```
<!DOCTYPE HTML PUBLIC "-//W3C//DTD HTML 4.01
    Frameset//EN"
    "http://www.w3.org/TR/html4/frameset.dtd">
    <HTML>
<HEAD><TITLE>Fleabag Kitty</TITLE></HEAD>
<BODY BGCOLOR="#3399CC">With a scratcha
    scratcha here and a scratcha scratcha
    there. . .
</BODY>
</HTML>
```

*2.* Add the TEXT="#FFFFFF" attribute to the <BODY> tag to change the color of the body text, as follows:

```
<BODY BGCOLOR="#3399CC" TEXT="#FFFFFF">With a
    scratcha scratcha here and a scratcha
    scratcha there. . .
</BODY>
```

The following figure shows the colored text on a background.

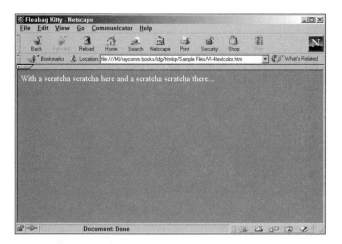

## Changing link colors

This example shows you how to change link colors on your Web page.

*Note:* This example builds on the previous one.

To change link colors on your Web page, use the following steps:

*1.* Start your HTML page, which should look something like this example:

```
<!DOCTYPE HTML PUBLIC "-//W3C//DTD HTML 4.01
    Frameset//EN"
    "http://www.w3.org/TR/html4/frameset.dtd">
    <HTML>
<HEAD><TITLE>Fleabag Kitty</TITLE></HEAD>
<BODY BGCOLOR="#3399CC" TEXT="#FFFFFF">With a
    scratcha scratcha here and a scratcha
    scratcha there. . .
</BODY>
</HTML>
```

*2.* Add LINK="#FF0000" attributes to the <BODY> tag to change the various link colors, as follows:

```
<BODY BGCOLOR="#3399CC" TEXT="#FFFFFF"
  LINK="#FF0000">With a scratcha scratcha here
  and a scratcha scratcha there. . .
</BODY>
```

3. Add ALINK="#FFFF00" and VLINK="#8C1717" attributes to
   the <BODY> tag to finish changing the link colors, as shown
   here:

```
<BODY BGCOLOR="#3399CC" TEXT="#FFFFFF"
  LINK="#FF0000" ALINK="#FFFF00"
  VLINK="#8C1717">With a scratcha scratcha
  here and a scratcha scratcha there. . .
</BODY>
```

After you add links to your document and browse through some of
them, you see the differences in link color, visited link color, and
active link color. Enjoy!

## Specifying Text Alignment

In addition to recoloring text and links, you can also move text
around so that it's not all aligned on the left. You can align headings, paragraphs, other text, and images by using the attributes in
the following table.

**See also** Part X for details on using style sheet alignment options.

Keep in mind that although most browsers support these attributes, not all do, so your text may not be aligned correctly in some
browsers. Always try out designs in more than one browser to
make sure that your design works the way you think it should.

The following table presents the attributes used to control text
alignment.

| HTML Attribute | Effect | Use in Pairs? |
|---|---|---|
| ALIGN="CENTER" | Centers text within the left and right margins. | No |
| ALIGN="RIGHT" | Aligns text on the right margin. | No |

You don't need to add an attribute if you want the element aligned
left. Browsers align text to the left unless you tell them to do
otherwise.

If you want to use center and right alignment for headings, paragraphs, and images, follow this example.

*Note:* Before beginning, make sure that you have your browser and text editor open and ready to create a new document. Or you can apply this information to an existing document.

Follow these steps:

1. Start your HTML page, which should look similar to the following example:

```
<!DOCTYPE HTML PUBLIC "-//W3C//DTD HTML 4.01
    Frameset//EN"
    "http://www.w3.org/TR/html4/frameset.dtd">
    <HTML>
<HEAD><TITLE>Birthday</TITLE></HEAD>
<BODY>
</BODY>
</HTML>
```

2. Type a heading, as follows:

```
<BODY>
<H1>Happy Birthday, Winchester</H1>
</BODY>
```

3. Add the ALIGN="right" attribute to the heading, as in the following example:

```
<H1 ALIGN="right">Happy Birthday,
    Winchester</H1>
```

4. Insert a graphic on the left side of the heading, as follows:

```
<H1 ALIGN="right"><IMG SRC="winch.jpg">Happy
    Birthday, Winchester</H1>
```

5. Type the following paragraph information:

```
<H1 ALIGN="right"><IMG SRC="winch.jpg">Happy
    Birthday, Winchester</H1>
<P>On March 3, Deb and Eric snuck up on their
    cat, Winchester, and surprised him with a
    water balloon for his birthday. It was lucky
    #13 for Winchester.</P>
</BODY>
```

6. Add the ALIGN="center" attribute to the paragraph, as shown here:

```
<P ALIGN="center">On March 3, Deb and Eric
    snuck up on their cat, Winchester, and
    surprised him with a water balloon for his
    birthday. It was lucky #13 for
    Winchester.</P>
```

The following figure shows the result.

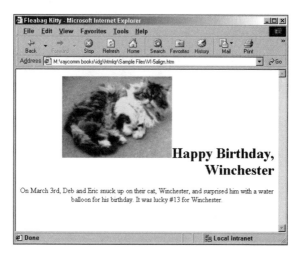

# Using Type Specifications

As we mention in The Big Picture earlier in this book, HTML was not designed to support specific formatting. HTML was conceived with the idea that authors would specify headings and lists, and readers (or the readers' browsers) would take care of applying fonts and sizes.

A generation of designers accustomed to desktop publishing and to being able to control every aspect of document design, however, sought out ways to control HTML design as well. In response, newer browsers and the most widely supported HTML specification provide some tags specifically to format text precisely.

The combination of "pure" HTML, without the formatting tags in this section, and style sheets (covered in Part X) provides the best of both worlds — HTML coding simplicity and complete layout and design control. Unfortunately, this HTML 4.0 combo is only an option if your readers use HTML 4.0-compliant browsers, such as Netscape Navigator 4.0 (sort of) or Microsoft Internet Explorer 4.0 or newer.

If you choose to use the formatting commands in this section, remember that not all browsers support them. Additionally, specifying fonts, in particular, carries no guarantee that your readers have the correct fonts or can display exactly what you want them to see. The following table shows the tags and attributes used to specify type characteristics.

| HTML Tag or Attribute | Effect | Use in Pairs? |
|---|---|---|
| `<FONT>...</FONT>` | Changes the font. | Yes |
| `COLOR="#rrggbb"` | Colors the text based on the rrggbb number. | No |
| `FACE="..."` | Sets the typeface NAME. A list of font names can be specified. | No |
| `SIZE="n"` | Changes the font size n on a scale from 1 to 7. | No |

**Note:** Before you begin, make sure that you have your browser and text editor open.

To change the characteristics of a specific block of text in the water balloons example, follow these steps:

1. Start your HTML document, which should look something like the following example:

```
<!DOCTYPE HTML PUBLIC "-//W3C//DTD HTML 4.01
    Transitional//EN"
    "http://www.w3.org/TR/html4/
    transitional.dtd"> <HTML>
<HEAD><TITLE>Making Effective Water
    Balloons</TITLE>
</HEAD>
<BODY>
<H1>Making Effective Water Balloons</H1>
<P>
Making water balloons is <EM>easy</EM>. . .
    but making <B>effective</B> water balloons
    takes time and patience. The result is a
    water balloon that does not break in your
    hand, offers <I>maximum splashing power</I>,
    and requires virtually no post-splat clean
    up.
</P>
</BODY>
</HTML>
```

2. Add the `<FONT>` tags around the text you want to change, as follows:

```
<H1>Making Effective Water Balloons</H1>
<P>
<FONT>
Making water balloons is <EM>easy</EM>. . .
    but making <B>effective</B> water balloons
    takes time and patience. The result is a
```

```
water balloon that does not break in your
hand, offers <I>maximum splashing power</I>,
and requires virtually no post-splat clean
up.
</FONT>
</P>
```

3. To change the size, add the appropriate SIZE= attribute to the font tag, as shown in the following example.

   By default, the size is 4. (The number does not represent any-thing — it just is.) You can specify a size relative to the default (+1 for one size larger or -2 for two sizes smaller) or in absolute numbers such as 1 or 7.

```
<FONT SIZE=+2>
Making water balloons is <EM>easy</EM>. . .
  but making <B>effective</B> water balloons
takes time and patience. The result is a
water balloon that does not break in your
hand, offers <I>maximum splashing power
</I>, and requires virtually no post-splat
clean up.
</FONT>
```

4. To change the typeface, add the FACE= attribute, as the follow-ing example shows.

   You can name any font on your system (bearing in mind that the font also must be available on your reader's system to appear correctly). You can also list fonts in descending order of preference. If the first isn't available, your reader's browser moves along to the next and next.

```
<FONT FACE="Gill Sans, Arial, Courier"
   SIZE=+2>
Making water balloons is <EM>easy</EM>. . .
  but making <B>effective</B> water balloons
takes time and patience. The result is a
water balloon that does not break in your
hand, offers <I>maximum splashing power
</I>, and requires virtually no post-splat
clean up.
</FONT>
```

The following figure shows the new typeface in a Web browser.

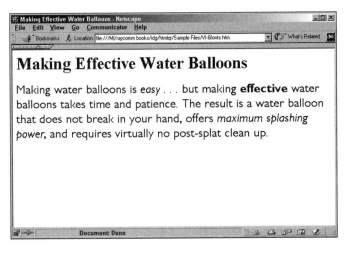

Reliable fonts for Windows include Arial, Times New Roman, and
Courier New. Helvetica and Times are similar to Arial and Times
New Roman and also are frequently available.

5. To change the color, add the COLOR= attribute, as shown in the
   following example.

   As with other text color settings (described earlier in this
   part), you use an #rrggbb number to specify the color.

   ```
   <FONT FACE="Gill Sans, Courier, Arial"
     COLOR="#000000" SIZE=+2>
   Making water balloons is <EM>easy</EM>. . .
      but making <B>effective</B> water balloons
      takes time and patience. The result is a
      water balloon that does not break in your
      hand, offers <I>maximum splashing power
      </I>, and requires virtually no post-splat
      clean up.
   </FONT>
   ```

# Serving HTML to the World

In Part VII, we introduce you to the task of placing your HTML documents on a server so that — potentially at least — anyone connected to the Internet can see your documents. Although this part gets a little technical in places, we assure you that it's not that bad. We also walk you through how to use some of the neat additional capabilities that a Web server gives you.

In several places, you will need to ask for help from your server administrator to find out how your Web server is organized and what is available for your use. Don't hesitate to get to know your server administrators. They can give you all kinds of useful information about the server and what's special about the way it's set up.

*See also* Part I for information about tags if you need a quick brushup on using them. In this part, we don't address tag basics — we just tell you to apply them.

## In this part . . .

About Servers  . . . . . . . . . . . . . . . . . . . . . . . . . . . . . 116
Determining Your URL  . . . . . . . . . . . . . . . . . . . . . . 116
Getting Documents onto the Server  . . . . . . . . . . 117
Getting Server Programs  . . . . . . . . . . . . . . . . . . . 118
Linking Things Automatically  . . . . . . . . . . . . . . . . 119
Including a Counter  . . . . . . . . . . . . . . . . . . . . . . . 120

# About Servers

*Servers* (also known as *HTML servers, http servers,* or *Web servers*) send HTML documents to any computer on the network that requests them. In most cases, servers are located on the Internet and serve documents to any other computer on the Net.

Sometimes servers are located on a corporate *intranet* and are accessible only from other computers in that corporation. No matter whether you're producing HTML pages for publication on the Internet or on a corporate intranet, you need to complete the following steps:

*1.* Prepare your documents.

*2.* Put them on the server.

*3.* Test the documents.

*4.* Enhance them with any server-specific capabilities (such as the ones we talk about in this part).

*5.* Put the documents on the server again.

*6.* Test them again (and feel free to repeat this step as often as you want).

As a rule, don't put anything on a server that you're not prepared for the entire world to see. Even if you don't think that people can see your handiwork (for example, because you don't have any links to that document), little information-seeking programs roam the Internet, and they can find it — particularly if they shouldn't.

Any computer on the network, even that PC on your desktop, can function as a Web server. Just how to set up Web servers is way beyond the scope of this book, but if your computer is always on and always connected to the Internet (or your local network), you can make it a Web server.

Check out *HTML 4 For Dummies,* 3rd Edition, by Ed Tittel, Natanya Pitts, and Chelsea Valentine (published by IDG Books Worldwide, Inc.), for more information about setting up Web servers.

# Determining Your URL

Your server has a specific name. It's probably something like www. company.com or www.organization.org, which means that the basic URL for pages on that server is http://www.company.com/ or http://www.organization.org/. Your server administrator probably gives you a directory or set of directories in which you put all the documents that you want to serve to the world.

You can obtain your URL from the Web administrator or possibly by reading documentation about your Web site. Don't bank on the documentation, however; Web servers are much too often poorly documented, and you may find that asking your administrator is easier than trying to find the answer yourself.

In all likelihood, if you have an account with an Internet Service Provider (ISP) your base URL ends up as `http://www.organization.com/~yourid/`, just as ours is `http://www.xmission.com/~ejray/`. Of course, in the place of your id, you have a real ID, which you use to sign onto the system. You can place all of the documents that you develop on the server in your account. Their absolute URLs start with your base URL and include all additional file or directory information.

***See also*** Part II for a review of URLs and files.

If you're paying big bucks for your Web site or if you're the Webmaster for your organization, you may have a URL such as `http://www.mysite.com/`, with `mysite` being your actual business. If you want to have your organization name appear in the server name, don't delay. Move quickly and ask your administrator about *virtual domains,* which give you the glory of your own name without the hassle of needing to maintain the server. The same information about putting your HTML documents on the server applies, but remember that going this way makes you look more expensive.

If you're the new Webmaster for your organization, good for you! The job's fun. (Really!) If that's your situation and we tell you to see your Webmaster for help, just find the server administrator or the head geek in your organization.

## Getting Documents onto the Server

Every time you make changes or updates to your documents, you must put those changes back on the server so that your readers can see them. Just as you've become used to making your changes in your document, saving it, and then clicking the reload key in your browser, you find a pattern to making changes to a document on the server. We suggest performing the following steps:

*1.* Make your changes.

*2.* Save your changes.

*3.* Upload your changes to the server.

*4.* Reload your browser to check out the changes.

How, you ask, do I get my documents on the server? You most likely use an *FTP* (file transfer protocol) program to put your documents on the server. Your server administrator can fill you in on the procedure. You may want to use WS-FTP or FTP Explorer (for Windows), Fetch (for Macintosh), or some form of plain FTP (mostly for UNIX) to transfer your files to the server. Many Web-authoring packages now also provide built-in file-transfer capabilities; check out Netscape Communicator on all platforms, as well as Microsoft's Web Publishing Wizard.

***See also*** The Big Picture for information about FTP programs.

# Getting Server Programs

Server programs are small additions to the actual Web server that allow you to do cool stuff. They're basically the things that differentiate between what you can do on your own computer and what you can do on the server. Finding out about server programs is pretty much a "see your server administrator" task.

An example of these programs are the little counters (which we discuss in the section "Including a Counter," later in this part) that record how many times people access your Web page. You can include a line in your HTML to tell the server to run the program, add one to the count, and display the total in your page. These programs, however, are sometimes a bit difficult to access.

You've probably noticed that server administrators are pretty tense about security (and justifiably so). Generally, you find very few directories on a server in which you can run a program for your Web pages. But if your administrator permits you to run a server program, such as the counter dealie we just mentioned, she must put that program in the right place on the system, such as the cgi-bin directory, which is where server programs traditionally live.

If you're doing your Web pages on a budget or if your server administrator is fairly busy, using existing programs is probably the only alternative. To find out what programs are available, ask your administrator the following questions:

- ✔ What programs are available in the cgi-bin (pronounced see-gee-eye-bin) directory?

- ✔ What do these programs do?

- ✔ How do I find their instructions?

- ✔ Whom do I call if the programs don't work?

# Linking Things Automatically

One time-saving tip is to automatically include information within your HTML documents. Just as many e-mail programs automatically affix a signature to the end of the message, you can have your HTML pages automatically include other documents.

Your server administrator must enable server-side includes before automatic links to information can work. A *server-side include* is a command that tells the server to include other information with the document being served.

These includes do have a downside — they slow the server somewhat. On the other hand, if you're inserting many graphics, your readers aren't going to notice the difference that a small include makes.

Some servers require that files with server-side includes have an extension of .shtml, rather than .html. This extension just helps the server know what's going on. Your server administrator can tell you whether this extension is necessary.

You can include many goodies. We recommend, however, that you stick to a couple of useful basics — the date and the time that the document was last modified. The following table shows some of the tags and attributes that can be included from many servers.

| HTML Tag or Attribute | Effect | Use in Pairs? |
|---|---|---|
| <!-- ...--> | Indicates a comment or server command. | No |
| #INCLUDE | Indicates to include a file. | No |
| FILE="..." | Indicates the filename relative to the directory. | No |
| VIRTUAL="..." | Indicates the filename relative to the server. | No |
| #ECHO VAR="..." | Indicates to display the value of a variable. | No |
| DATE_LOCAL | Indicates that the variable to display is the local date. | No |
| LAST_MODIFIED | Indicates that the variable to display is the last time the document was changed. | No |

If, for example, your company is prone to takeovers and you fear that you may spend the next three years changing and rechanging the company name in all your Web pages, you can automate the process so that you need to make a change only once; it then shows up in all your pages. Use the following steps to perform that task:

1. Create a new HTML document that contains the name of the company.

   In this document, do not use the `<HEAD>`, `<BODY>`, or `<HTML>` tags — just type the name of the company.

2. Enter `<!--#include file="companyname.html"-->` in every other document where you want to include the company name.

3. Upload both the documents — one with the company name, one (or more) with the cryptic command — to the server.

   You should find the company name right where it belongs in the second file. (If you view your document from your computer, you can't see anything in this place.)

You can go back and change the `companyname.html` file to reflect the new name, and you're back in business (so to speak). You can include a file in as many other documents as you want. Granted, using just the company name isn't that impressive, but if you take these steps to automatically include all the information you repeat verbatim on several pages, you're going to be in great shape. Think of what you can do with the company name, address, phone number, president's name, and so on.

# Including a Counter

As we mention earlier, a counter is that little feature that tells you how many people have visited an HTML document. Keep in mind that using a counter is a mixed bag — sometimes you may not want everyone to know how many (or how few) people visit your pages.

This example shows you how to include a counter in your Web page.

*Note:* Before you add a counter, you must have an existing HTML document to which to add the counter. We assume that your document is ready to go.

You need to contact your server administrator and ask what code to use to place a counter in your document. Our administrator said that the magic phrase is `<!--#exec cgi="/cgi-bin/counter"-->`.

To include a counter in your Web page, follow these basic steps:

*1.* Start with a basic HTML document, similar to the following:

```
<!DOCTYPE HTML PUBLIC "-//W3C//DTD HTML 4.01
    Frameset//EN"
    "http://www.w3.org/TR/html4/frameset.dtd">
<HTML>
<HEAD><TITLE>Lucy Counts, Too</TITLE></HEAD>
<BODY>
<H1>Lucy Counts, Too</H1>
<P>This page is dedicated to Lucy, who is less
    gross and more cute than Winchester. <B>
people have visited this page.</B></P>
</BODY>
</HTML>
```

*2.* Add the counter tag at the place where you want the number, as follows.

(Make sure that you leave a space on each side so that the counter doesn't run into the text.)

```
<!DOCTYPE HTML PUBLIC "-//W3C//DTD HTML 4.01
    Frameset//EN"
    "http://www.w3.org/TR/html4/frameset.dtd">
<HTML>
<HEAD><TITLE>Lucy Counts, Too</TITLE></HEAD>
<BODY>
<H1>Lucy Counts, Too</H1>
<P>This page is dedicated to Lucy, who is less
    gross and more cute than Winchester. <B>
<!--#exec cgi="/cgi-bin/counter"-->
people have visited this page.</B></P>
</BODY>
</HTML>
```

*3.* Save and then upload your document to the server and check it out.

You then see something similar to the following figure.

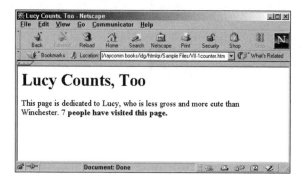

# Developing Forms

In Part VIII, we introduce forms, which you might think of as online versions of hard-copy forms that have check boxes and blanks to fill in, among other possible features. These online forms can help you get feedback and information from readers, as well as provide an interactive component to your Web site.

To develop a form for your Web site, you need the help of your server administrator. In this chapter, we tell you where you will need to ask for help, as well as tell you what information to request.

With that, let's take a look. . .

## In this part . . .

Creating a Basic Form . . . . . . . . . . . . . . . . . . . . . . . 124

Including Form Components . . . . . . . . . . . . . . . . . 126

# Creating a Basic Form

In HTML, forms are just what they are in real life — a fairly impersonal, pretty effective means of getting standardized information from other people. You may use forms to facilitate the following tasks:

✔ Conduct a survey.

✔ Collect addresses or information about visitors to your HTML pages.

✔ Allow people to register for something.

The following table shows the basic ⟨FORM⟩ tags and attributes that you use.

| HTML Tag or Attribute | Effect | Use in Pairs? |
|---|---|---|
| ⟨FORM...⟩ ... ⟨/FORM⟩ | Encloses the entire form. | Yes |
| ACTION="..." | Identifies what should happen to the data after the form is submitted. | No |
| METHOD="..." | Identifies methods; valid options are GET or POST— one is required. | No |

Notice that in creating forms, you need to make sure that the information gets back to you after the reader fills out the form and clicks submit. Although form results can be processed and returned in various ways, your server administrator will most likely have the server set up to e-mail form results directly to you.

The basic ⟨FORM⟩ tag is a two-parter, having both an initial tag and a closing tag. You can use the ⟨FORM⟩ tag to have information sent back to you directly or to a program that compiles the information for you.

The ⟨FORM⟩ tag has two primary (essential) attributes, ACTION and METHOD. The ACTION attribute tells the server what to do with the information once the server receives it. The METHOD attribute tells the server how to get the processed information back to you. Exactly what you fill in as values for these two attributes depends on what your server administrator tells you. So, before you get started creating your form, go ahead and contact your server administrator and tell her that you want to create a form that can be e-mailed to your personal address and ask what you should fill in for the ACTION and METHOD attributes.

For example, our administrator told us to use the following elements:

```
ACTION="http://www.raycomm.com/
   cgi-bin/email?raycomm"
Method=POST
```

Notice that the rest of our examples are constructed based on this information. Just ask your server administrator exactly what to use (or where to look for instructions).

So, time to get started creating a form. We assume that the following information is true:

- ✔ You've already contacted your server administrator and gotten the ACTION and METHOD information.

- ✔ You have your HTML document open in an editing program.

- ✔ You've opened the HTML document in your browser so that you can view and test the document.

- ✔ You completely understand that we never do anything to hurt cats.

To include a form in your Web page, follow these basic steps:

*1.* Start with a basic HTML document, similar to this one:

```
<!DOCTYPE HTML PUBLIC "-//W3C//DTD HTML 4.01
   Frameset//EN"
   "http://www.w3.org/TR/html4/frameset.dtd">
<HTML>
<HEAD><TITLE>Survey: How to Get the
   Cats</TITLE></HEAD>
<BODY>
<H1>Survey: How to Get the Cats</H1>
<P>We've decided to take a survey about the
   best pranks to play on the cats. Please
   complete the survey and click the Submit
   button.</P>
</BODY>
</HTML>
```

*2.* Add the <FORM> and </FORM> tags to show where the form goes, as follows:

```
Please complete the survey and click the Submit
   button.</P>
<FORM>
</FORM>
</BODY>
</HTML>
```

**3.** Add the information that your server administrator gave you for the ACTION and METHOD attributes. Remember, shown here is what our administrator told us to fill in:

```
<FORM METHOD="POST"
    ACTION="http://www.raycomm.com/
    cgi-bin/email?raycomm">
</FORM>
```

The following figure shows the basic document.

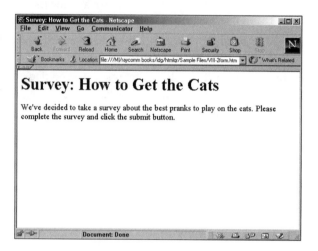

At this point, you can't see anything different about your page. Nor can you test the page to find out whether it works. Just forge ahead, finish up the form, and satisfy your curiosity.

## Including Form Components

If you have the basics of the form under control, you now want to include some <INPUT> fields so that you can start collecting information. The basic form-input tags shown in the following table, in many permutations, should carry you through the next several sections.

| HTML Tag or Attribute | Effect | Use in Pairs? |
|---|---|---|
| `<INPUT...>` | Identifies some type of input field. | No |
| `CHECKED` | Shows which item is selected by default (check box/radio button). | No |
| `MAXLENGTH=n` | Indicates the maximum number of characters in the field width. | No |
| `NAME="..."` | Indicates the name of the field. | No |
| `SIZE=n` | Displays field characters wide. | No |
| `TYPE="..."` | Indicates the type of field. Valid types are `TEXT`, `PASSWORD`, `CHECKBOX`, `RADIO`, `SUBMIT`, `RESET`, `FILE`, `IMAGE`, `BUTTON`, and `HIDDEN`. | No |
| `VALUE="..."` | Indicates value of button (and the label for Submit and Reset). | No |

## Including Submit and Reset buttons

Now that you've created the form, you need to add Submit and Reset buttons that the readers click to submit the form (or start over again if they goof up). The Submit button sends the information in after your readers click it, whereas the Reset button just clears the input from the form.

To include Submit and Reset buttons, enter the following text and tags in your HTML document.

**Remember:** You need a functional form before you start adding Submit and Reset buttons.

```
<FORM METHOD="POST" ACTION="http://www.raycomm.com/
   cgi-bin/email?raycomm">
<INPUT TYPE="SUBMIT" VALUE="Submit">
<INPUT TYPE="RESET" VALUE="Reset">
</FORM>
```

The following figure shows these two buttons in your HTML document.

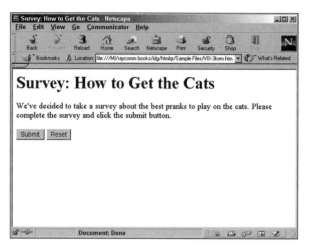

The VALUE attributes determine what text appears on the buttons.

So, for example, you can change the VALUE of the TYPE="RESET" button to read "Forget it!" if you want to add some zest. The full tag then looks as follows:

`<INPUT TYPE="RESET" VALUE="Forget it!">`

HTML 4.0 (but only HTML 4.0 and newer) supports another tag, logically called <BUTTON>, to put other types of buttons in your documents. These buttons work best in conjunction with JavaScript scripts to do things like checking the form for accuracy before submitting it. See Appendix A for information about using the <BUTTON> tag and refer to *JavaScript For Dummies Quick Reference,* by Emily A. Vander Veer, published by IDG Books Worldwide, Inc., for everything you need to know to get started with JavaScript.

## Including check boxes, radio buttons, and more

Check boxes and radio buttons are the objects that users can click to select choices from a list. Check boxes allow you to select multiple options. Radio buttons are designed so that you can choose one from a list — just like with pushing buttons on a car radio. Both check boxes and radio buttons are variations on the <INPUT> field. The following figure shows examples of both.

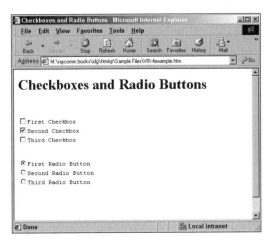

## Making check boxes

Making check boxes is not complicated — you use several tags, but the process is the same as creating anything else with HTML.

This example shows you how to use check boxes in your document.

*Note:* You need to have a functional form, including Submit and Reset buttons, before you add check boxes. You start with the following example — just a section of a complete document — and build on it. (And remember — we dearly love our cats and really wouldn't ever surprise them with a balloon — water or otherwise.)

```
<FORM METHOD="POST"
    ACTION="http://www.raycomm.com/
    cgi-bin/email?raycomm">
<INPUT TYPE="SUBMIT" VALUE="Submit">
<INPUT TYPE="RESET" VALUE="Reset">
</FORM>
```

To use check boxes in your document, follow these steps:

*1.* Enter an `<INPUT>` tag on the blank line after the beginning of the form, as follows:

```
<FORM METHOD="POST"
    ACTION="http://www.raycomm.com/
    cgi-bin/email?raycomm">
<INPUT>
<INPUT TYPE="SUBMIT" VALUE="Submit">
<INPUT TYPE="RESET"VALUE="Reset">
</FORM>
```

2. Identify the type that you want to use, as shown in the following example.

   (We start with a check box.)

   ```
   <FORM METHOD="POST"
      ACTION="http://www.raycomm.com/
      cgi-bin/email?raycomm">
   <INPUT TYPE="CHECKBOX">
   <INPUT TYPE="SUBMIT" VALUE="Submit">
   <INPUT TYPE="RESET" VALUE="Reset">
   </FORM>
   ```

3. Insert the text that you want people to see behind that check
   box, as follows.

   (Until you do so, they see a check box with no description.)

   ```
   <FORM METHOD="POST"
      ACTION="http://www.raycomm.com/
      cgi-bin/email?raycomm">
   <INPUT TYPE="CHECKBOX">Throw a balloon!
   <INPUT TYPE="SUBMIT" VALUE="Submit">
   <INPUT TYPE="RESET" VALUE="Reset">
   </FORM>
   ```

4. Identify the name of the <INPUT> field, as shown here.

   (You see this field as you're reading the input from your form.
   Make the name something short and logical.)

   ```
   <FORM METHOD="POST"
      ACTION="http://www.raycomm.com/
      cgi-bin/email?raycomm">
   <INPUT TYPE="CHECKBOX" NAME="Throw">
      Throw a balloon!
   <INPUT TYPE="SUBMIT" VALUE="Submit">
   <INPUT TYPE="RESET" VALUE="Reset">
   </FORM>
   ```

5. Enter the text that you want to see if someone selects this
   option, as shown in the following example.

   ***Remember:*** Whenever you see the output of this form, it's
   probably as an e-mail message with just words in the place of
   the pretty check marks, so you can't look at the checks. We
   recommend something similar to the NAME attribute. Make this
   one short and to the point.

   ```
   <FORM METHOD="POST"
      ACTION="http://www.raycomm.com/
      cgi-bin/email?raycomm">
   ```

```
<INPUT TYPE="CHECKBOX" NAME="Throw"
   VALUE="ThrowBalloon"> Throw a balloon!
<INPUT TYPE="SUBMIT" VALUE="Submit">
<INPUT TYPE="RESET" VALUE="Reset">
</FORM>
```

**6.** Enter a couple more lines to complete the list, as follows (because you probably don't want a check box list with only one thing to check).

(We also added a <P> tag at the end to force a new line.)

```
<FORM METHOD="POST"
   ACTION="http://www.raycomm.com/
   cgi-bin/email?raycomm">
<INPUT TYPE="CHECKBOX" NAME="Throw"
   VALUE="ThrowBalloon"> Throw a balloon!
<INPUT TYPE="CHECKBOX" NAME="Hurl"
   VALUE="HurlBalloon"> Hurl a balloon!
<INPUT TYPE="CHECKBOX" NAME="Lob"
   VALUE="LobBalloon"> Lob a balloon!<P>
<INPUT TYPE="SUBMIT" VALUE="Submit">
<INPUT TYPE="RESET" VALUE="Reset">
</FORM>
```

**7.** Enter a CHECKED attribute in the check box that you want to have selected by default, as in the following example.

(Do so if you want to select a check box in advance to give a recommendation or to make sure that something gets checked.)

```
<FORM METHOD="POST"
   ACTION="http://www.raycomm.com/
   cgi-bin/email?raycomm">
<INPUT TYPE="CHECKBOX" NAME="Throw"
   VALUE="ThrowBalloon"> Throw a balloon!
<INPUT CHECKED TYPE="CHECKBOX" NAME="Hurl"
   VALUE="HurlBalloon"> Hurl a balloon!
<INPUT TYPE="CHECKBOX" NAME="Lob"
   VALUE="LobBalloon"> Lob a balloon!<P>
<INPUT TYPE="SUBMIT" VALUE="Submit">
<INPUT TYPE="RESET" VALUE="Reset">
</FORM>
```

The following figure shows the form with the addition of check boxes.

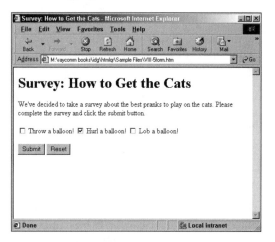

## Making radio buttons

Making radio buttons is similar to making check boxes — you use several tags, and the process is the same as that for using other HTML tags.

This example shows you how to include radio buttons in your form.

*Note:* Before you start making radio buttons, make sure that you already have your functional form completed. This example uses the following form (developed in other examples in this chapter):

```
<FORM METHOD="POST"
   ACTION="http://www.raycomm.com/
   cgi-bin/email?raycomm">
<INPUT TYPE="CHECKBOX" NAME="Throw"
   VALUE="ThrowBalloon"> Throw a balloon!
<INPUT CHECKED TYPE="CHECKBOX" NAME="Hurl"
   VALUE="HurlBalloon"> Hurl a balloon!
<INPUT TYPE="CHECKBOX" NAME="Lob"
   VALUE="LobBalloon"> Lob a balloon!<P>
<INPUT TYPE="SUBMIT" VALUE="Submit">
<INPUT TYPE="RESET" VALUE="Reset">
</FORM>
```

To include radio buttons in your form, follow these steps:

*1.* Insert the `<INPUT>` tag and the text that people should see, as follows:

```
<INPUT>Do it--it'll be funny!
<INPUT TYPE="SUBMIT" VALUE="Submit">
```

```
<INPUT TYPE="RESET" VALUE="Reset">
</FORM>
```

**2.** Add the TYPE indicator to show that it is a radio button, as
shown here:

```
<INPUT TYPE="RADIO">Do it--it'll be funny!
```

**3.** Add the NAME indicator, as follows.

(The NAME applies to the whole set of radio buttons, so we've
chosen a less specific name.)

```
<INPUT TYPE="RADIO" NAME="Prank">Do it--it'll
    be funny!
```

**4.** Add the VALUE attribute, as in the following example.

(Again, this value is what you see after you get the input of the
form back, so make this value unique to this choice and make
it descriptive.)

```
<INPUT TYPE="RADIO" NAME="Prank" VALUE="Do">
    Do it--it'll be funny!
```

**5.** Add the CHECKED attribute again, as follows because this
selection is the recommended choice:

```
<INPUT TYPE="RADIO" NAME="Prank" VALUE="Do"
CHECKED>Do it--it'll be funny!
```

**6.** Add as many more radio buttons to this set as you want, along
with line breaks (<BR> or <P>) between them just to make
them look nice, as shown here.

(*Remember:* Radio buttons are designed to accept only one
selection from the group, so make sure that they all share the
same NAME field. This way, the computer knows that they
belong together.)

```
<INPUT TYPE="RADIO" NAME="Prank" VALUE="Do"
    CHECKED>Do it--it'll be funny!<BR>
<INPUT TYPE="RADIO" NAME="Prank" VALUE="DoNot">
    Don't play a prank, meanie!<BR>
<INPUT TYPE="RADIO" NAME="Prank"
    VALUE="DoNotCare">I couldn't care less.
    They're your cats, and you'll have to live
    with yourself.<P>
```

The following figure shows the addition of radio buttons to the
form.

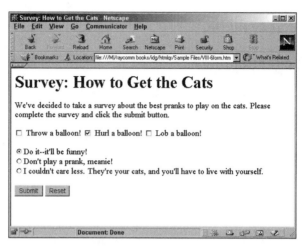

If you're testing your form and you find that the CHECKED attribute doesn't seem to be working, click the Reset button within your form. (If you're following along, remember that a previous example explained how to change the Reset button to say "Forget it.")

## Using other input types

Other input types, such as TEXT, can be very useful. TEXT allows you to insert a small amount of information (such as a name or an address) into your form.

This example shows you how to include text-input areas in your form.

*Note:* Before you start adding other input attributes, make sure that you already have your functional form completed. This example uses the following form (developed in other examples in this chapter):

```
<FORM METHOD="POST"
   ACTION="http://www.raycomm.com/
   cgi-bin/email?raycomm">
<INPUT TYPE="CHECKBOX" NAME="Throw"
   VALUE="ThrowBalloon"> Throw a balloon!
<INPUT CHECKED TYPE="CHECKBOX" NAME="Hurl"
   VALUE="HurlBalloon"> Hurl a balloon!
<INPUT TYPE="CHECKBOX" NAME="Lob"
   VALUE="LobBalloon"> Lob a balloon!<P>
<INPUT TYPE="RADIO" NAME="Prank" VALUE="Do"
   CHECKED>Do it--it'll be funny!<BR>
```

```
<INPUT TYPE="RADIO" NAME="Prank"
  VALUE="DoNot">Don't play a prank,
  meanie!<BR>
<INPUT TYPE="RADIO" NAME="Prank"
  VALUE="DoNotCare">I couldn't care less.
  They're your cats, and you'll have to live
  with yourself.<P>
<INPUT TYPE="SUBMIT" VALUE="Submit">
<INPUT TYPE="RESET" VALUE="Reset">
</FORM>
```

You're going to add the input area to the form that you've been developing, so check the previous section for context, if necessary.

To include text input areas in your form, follow these steps:

**1.** Insert the `<INPUT>` tag and the text that people should see, plus a tag (`<BR>` or `<P>`) to force a new line, as follows:

```
<INPUT>Your Name<P>
<INPUT TYPE="SUBMIT" VALUE="Submit">
<INPUT TYPE="RESET" VALUE="Reset">
</FORM>
```

**2.** Add the TYPE indicator to show that it is a text input area, as shown here:

```
<INPUT TYPE="TEXT">Your Name<P>
```

**3.** Add the NAME indicator, as follows:

```
<INPUT TYPE="TEXT" NAME="name">Your Name<P>
```

**4.** Add the SIZE indicator to tell the field how many characters wide it should be, as shown here:

```
<INPUT SIZE=35 TYPE="TEXT" NAME="name">Your
  Name<P>
```

The following figure shows the addition of the text input field to your form.

Survey: How to Get the Cats - Netscape

File  Edit  View  Go  Communicator  Help

Back  Forward  Reload  Home  Search  Netscape  Print  Security  Shop  Stop

Bookmarks  Location: file:///M/raycomm books/idg/htmlqr/Sample Files/VIII-7form.htm  What's Related

## Survey: How to Get the Cats

We've decided to take a survey about the best pranks to play on the cats. Please complete the survey and click the submit button.

☐ Throw a balloon!  ☑ Hurl a balloon!  ☐ Lob a balloon!

⦿ Do it--it'll be funny!
○ Don't play a prank, meanie!
○ I couldn't care less. They're your cats, and you'll have to live with yourself.

[                            ] Your Name

[ Submit ]  [ Reset ]

Document: Done

Other input types can also be pretty useful. You can, for example, insert a password-type field if you think your readers may want to make sure that their entry isn't visible to anyone. Just replace the TYPE=TEXT attribute with TYPE=PASSWORD.

If you develop many forms, you may also find it useful to have information submitted with the form that your readers don't see. You can include the purpose for the form, for example, as a VALUE so that it's sent back to you. You do so by adding a VALUE and changing the TYPE=TEXT attribute to TYPE=HIDDEN. The readers can't see the form field, but you can after you get the results of the form. Your code looks as follows:

```
<INPUT NAME="note" VALUE="Nonsense" TYPE=HIDDEN>
```

## Including select lists

Select lists are lists from which your readers can choose one or more items. They're like the font selection drop-down list in your word processing program.

The following table shows the tags and attributes used to include select lists in your HTML document.

| HTML Tag or Attribute | Effect | Use in Pairs? |
|---|---|---|
| `<SELECT...>` `... </SELECT>` | Provides a list of items to select. | Yes |
| *MULTIPLE* | Indicates that multiple selections are allowed. | No |

| HTML Tag or Attribute | Effect | Use in Pairs? |
|---|---|---|
| NAME="..." | Indicates the name of the field. | No |
| SIZE=n | Determines the size of the scrollable list by showing n options. | No |
| <OPTION...> | Precedes each item in an option list. | Yes, optionally |
| SELECTED | Identifies which option is selected. | No by default. |
| VALUE="..." | Indicates the value of the field. | No |

This example shows you how to add a select list to your form.

*Note:* Before including select lists, make sure that you already have a functional form completed. This example uses the following form (developed in other examples in this chapter):

```
<FORM METHOD="POST" ACTION="http://www.raycomm.com/
    cgi-bin/email?raycomm">
<INPUT TYPE="CHECKBOX" NAME="Throw"
    VALUE="ThrowBalloon"> Throw a balloon!
<INPUT CHECKED TYPE="CHECKBOX" NAME="Hurl"
    VALUE="HurlBalloon"> Hurl a balloon!
<INPUT TYPE="CHECKBOX" NAME="Lob"
    VALUE="LobBalloon"> Lob a balloon!<P>
<INPUT TYPE="RADIO" NAME="Prank" VALUE="Do"
    CHECKED>Do it--it'll be funny!<BR>
<INPUT TYPE="RADIO" NAME="Prank"
    VALUE="DoNot">Don't play a prank, meanie!<BR>
<INPUT TYPE="RADIO" NAME="Prank"
    VALUE="DoNotCare">I couldn't care less.
    They're your cats, and you'll have to live
    with yourself.<P>
<INPUT SIZE=35 TYPE="TEXT" NAME="name">Your Name<P>
<INPUT TYPE="SUBMIT" VALUE="Submit">
<INPUT TYPE="RESET" VALUE="Reset">
</FORM>
```

To add a select list to your form, follow these steps:

*1.* Insert the <SELECT> tags into your document and a tag (<BR> or <P>) to force a new line, as follows:

```
<SELECT>
</SELECT><P>
<INPUT TYPE="SUBMIT" VALUE="Submit">
<INPUT TYPE="RESET" VALUE="Reset">
</FORM>
```

**2.** Add the `NAME` attribute to the `<SELECT>` tag, as shown here.

(The `NAME` should be appropriately broad to cover the spectrum of choices.)

```
<SELECT NAME="Method">
</SELECT><P>
```

**3.** Add an `<OPTION>` that your readers can select, as follows:

```
<SELECT NAME="Method">
<OPTION VALUE="single">Single Balloon
</SELECT><P>
```

**4.** Complete your `<SELECT>` section by adding the other possible choices, as shown in the following example:

```
<SELECT NAME="Method">
<OPTION VALUE="single">Single Balloon
<OPTION VALUE="multiple">Multiple Balloons
<OPTION VALUE="hose">Just Use the Hose
</SELECT><P>
```

The following figure shows the addition of the select list to your form.

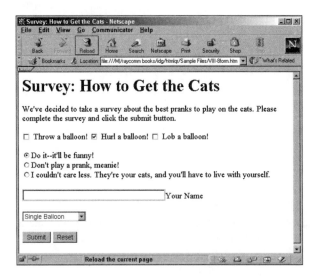

Don't underestimate the flexibility of your select list. You can add a `SIZE=3` attribute to the `<SELECT>` tag, for example, so that three items are visible at once. Your opening `<SELECT>` tag now looks as follows: `<SELECT SIZE=3 NAME="Method">`.

To allow people to select more than one item in your area, just add MULTIPLE to the opening <SELECT> tag. People can then click multiple items to make multiple selections, as shown in the following figure.

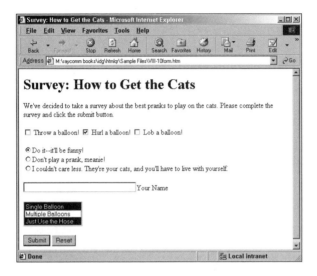

## Including text areas

Text areas are open spaces in your form in which your readers can type comments or enter other information.

The following table shows the tags and attributes used to add text areas to your form.

| HTML Tag or Attribute | Effect | Use in Pairs? |
|---|---|---|
| <TEXTAREA ...> ...</TEXTAREA> | Encloses a multiline text field. The enclosed text is the value displayed in the field. | Yes |
| COLS=n | Indicates the number of columns in the field. | No |
| NAME=" ... " | Indicates the name of the field. | No |
| ROWS=n | Indicates the number of rows in the field. | No |

This example shows you how to add a text area to your form.

***Note:*** You need to have a functional form, including Submit and Reset buttons, before you add <TEXTAREA> tags. We start with the following example — developed in other examples in this part — and build on it:

```
<FORM METHOD="POST" ACTION="http://www.raycomm.com/
    cgi-bin/email?raycomm">
<INPUT TYPE="CHECKBOX" NAME="Throw"
    VALUE="ThrowBalloon"> Throw a balloon!
<INPUT CHECKED TYPE="CHECKBOX" NAME="Hurl"
    VALUE="HurlBalloon"> Hurl a balloon!
<INPUT TYPE="CHECKBOX" NAME="Lob"
    VALUE="LobBalloon"> Lob a balloon!<P>
<INPUT TYPE="RADIO" NAME="Prank" VALUE="Do"
    CHECKED>Do it--it'll be funny!<BR>
<INPUT TYPE="RADIO" NAME="Prank"
    VALUE="DoNot">Don't play a prank, meanie!<BR>
<INPUT TYPE="RADIO" NAME="Prank"
    VALUE="DoNotCare">I couldn't care less.
    They're your cats, and you'll have to live
    with yourself.<P>
<INPUT SIZE=35 TYPE="TEXT" NAME="name">Your Name<P>
<SELECT SIZE=3 MULTIPLE NAME="Method">
<OPTION VALUE="single">Single Balloon
<OPTION VALUE="multiple">Multiple Balloons
<OPTION VALUE="hose">Just Use the Hose
</SELECT><P>
<INPUT TYPE="SUBMIT" VALUE="Submit">
<INPUT TYPE="RESET" VALUE="Reset">
</FORM>
```

To add a text area to your form, use the following steps:

*1.* Insert the <TEXTAREA> tags into your document and a tag (<P> or <BR>) to force a line break after the area, as follows:

```
<TEXTAREA>
</TEXTAREA><P>
<INPUT TYPE="SUBMIT" VALUE="Submit">
<INPUT TYPE="RESET" VALUE="Reset">
</FORM>
```

*2.* Add the NAME attribute to the tag, as shown here:

```
<TEXTAREA NAME="comments">
</TEXTAREA><P>
```

*3.* Add the ROWS and COLS attributes to set the size of the area, as in the following example:

```
<TEXTAREA NAME="comments" ROWS=3 COLS=40>
</TEXTAREA><P>
```

To include an example of suggested comments or to just tell people that they're really supposed to enter something, you can include the sample text between the `<TEXTAREA>` and `</TEXTAREA>` tags. You end up with source code and output similar to the following examples:

```
<TEXTAREA NAME="comments" ROWS=3 COLS=40>
Enter your comments here.
</TEXTAREA><P>
```

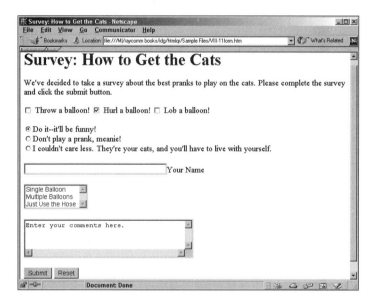

Size the text area appropriately for the information that you're trying to collect. Make the "What do you like about this page?" area, for example, much bigger than the "How do you really think we should treat our cats?" area.

## Including fieldsets and legends

`<FIELDSET>` and `<LEGEND>` tags can help make your forms more friendly and accommodating, particularly to nongraphical browsers. The `<FIELDSET>` tag groups sections of the form together (like personal information or questions on a specific topic), and the `<LEGEND>` tag provides a label for the group.

These tags are only supported by HTML 4.0-compliant browsers, so they won't show up in older browsers. However, they will also do no harm in older browsers, so there's no reason not to use them.

The following table shows the tags and attributes used to add field-sets and legends to your form.

| HTML Tag or Attribute | Effect | Use in Pairs? |
|---|---|---|
| `<FIELDSET>...` `</FIELDSET>` | Encloses a logical group of fields. | Yes |
| `<LEGEND>...` `</LEGEND>` | Provides a label or caption for a fieldset. | Yes |
| `ALIGN="..."` | Indicates alignment of the legend as `TOP`, `BOTTOM`, `LEFT`, or `RIGHT`. | No |

This example shows you how to add a fieldset and legend to your form.

*Note:* You need to have a functional form, including functional fields, before you add `<FIELDSET>` and `<LEGEND>` tags. We start with the following example — developed in other examples in this part — and build on it:

```
<FORM METHOD="POST" ACTION="http://www.raycomm.com/
    cgi-bin/email?raycomm">
<INPUT TYPE="CHECKBOX" NAME="Throw"
    VALUE="ThrowBalloon"> Throw a balloon!
<INPUT CHECKED TYPE="CHECKBOX" NAME="Hurl"
    VALUE="HurlBalloon"> Hurl a balloon!
<INPUT TYPE="CHECKBOX" NAME="Lob"
    VALUE="LobBalloon"> Lob a balloon!<P>
<INPUT TYPE="RADIO" NAME="Prank" VALUE="Do"
    CHECKED>Do it--it'll be funny!<BR>
<INPUT TYPE="RADIO" NAME="Prank"
    VALUE="DoNot">Don't play a prank, meanie!<BR>
<INPUT TYPE="RADIO" NAME="Prank"
    VALUE="DoNotCare">I couldn't care less.
    They're your cats, and you'll have to live
    with yourself.<P>
<INPUT SIZE=35 TYPE="TEXT" NAME="name">Your Name<P>
<SELECT SIZE=3 MULTIPLE NAME="Method">
<OPTION VALUE="single">Single Balloon
<OPTION VALUE="multiple">Multiple Balloons
<OPTION VALUE="hose">Just Use the Hose
</SELECT><P>
```

```
<TEXTAREA NAME="comments" ROWS=3 COLS=40>
Enter your comments here.
</TEXTAREA><P>
<INPUT TYPE="SUBMIT" VALUE="Submit">
<INPUT TYPE="RESET" VALUE="Reset">
</FORM>
```

To add a <FIELDSET> tag to your form, use the following steps:

**1.** Insert the <FIELDSET> tags into your document around a logical grouping of fields.

```
<FIELDSET>
<INPUT TYPE="CHECKBOX" NAME="Throw"
  VALUE="ThrowBalloon"> Throw a balloon!
<INPUT CHECKED TYPE="CHECKBOX" NAME="Hurl"
  VALUE="HurlBalloon"> Hurl a balloon!
<INPUT TYPE="CHECKBOX" NAME="Lob"
  VALUE="LobBalloon"> Lob a balloon!<P>
</FIELDSET>
```

**2.** Insert the <LEGEND> tags into your document just after the opening <FIELDSET> tag. Also, add a <BR> tag after the closing </LEGEND> tag to help accommodate older browsers (so that everything doesn't show up on a single line).

```
<FIELDSET>
<LEGEND></LEGEND><BR>
<INPUT TYPE="CHECKBOX" NAME="Throw"
  VALUE="ThrowBalloon"> Throw a balloon!
```

**3.** Add the legend text between the legend tags.

```
<FIELDSET>
<LEGEND>Prank Technique Questions</LEGEND><BR>
<INPUT TYPE="CHECKBOX" NAME="Throw"
  VALUE="ThrowBalloon"> Throw a balloon!
```

In an HTML 4.0-compliant browser, the legend looks really attractive, as shown in the top of the following figure. Even in other browsers, it isn't bad, as shown in the bottom of the same figure.

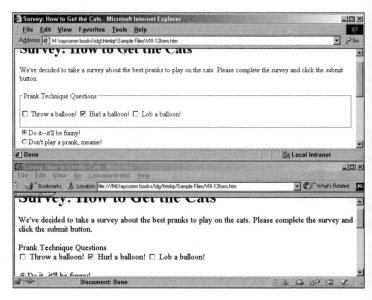

# Framing Your Site

In Part IX, we step into a whole new realm of HTML: *frames.* Frames let you have several different HTML documents visible within a single browser window, providing at least the possibility for visually interesting or easy-to-navigate sites. Of course, a framed site also makes you look like the HTML pro that you are.

Frames can get a little confusing at times, and the troubleshooting process isn't always the easiest. If you've gotten this far with HTML, however, nothing in here should be a real problem. Just take things one step at a time.

*See also* Part I for information about tags if you need a quick brushup on using them. In this part, we don't address tag basics — we just tell you to apply them.

## In this part . . .

About Frames . . . . . . . . . . . . . . . . . . . . . . . . . . . . . . . 146

Developing Content . . . . . . . . . . . . . . . . . . . . . . . . . . 148

Developing Alternative Content . . . . . . . . . . . . . . 149

Establishing the Frameset Document . . . . . . . . . . 149

Setting Up the Frames . . . . . . . . . . . . . . . . . . . . . . . 152

Setting Up Links and Targets . . . . . . . . . . . . . . . . 154

Testing Your Framed Site . . . . . . . . . . . . . . . . . . . . 155

# *About Frames*

*Frames* divide a browser window into several parts, just as a window (the glass kind) can be divided into several panes. Each frame (or pane) consists of an individual HTML document. In effect, using frames lets you put multiple separate HTML documents on a single page, each in an individual box.

You can use frames to create a variety of layouts. You may, for example, have seen frames used as a navigational aid, such as a frame with links on the left side of the browser window, as shown in the following figure.

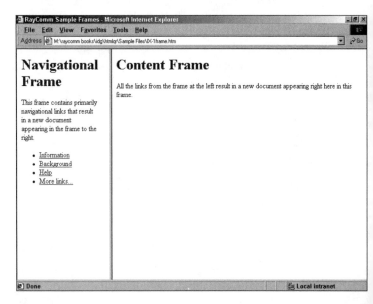

After readers select a link from the left frame, the linked document appears in the right frame — thus the navigational features stay visible at all times.

Or you may have seen frames used to help promote a corporate name or image. The logo and information, for example, appear in the top frame, and the linked documents appear in the bottom frame, as shown in the following figure.

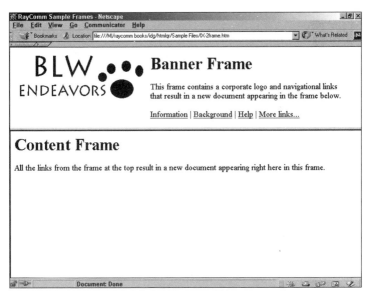

Think of these frames as being a two-column or two-row table. In these examples, the smaller of the two frames stays constant on the Web page (we call this the *navigation* or *banner document*), whereas the larger frame changes to display various HTML documents in the site (we call these the *content documents*). The effect is that you can develop the banner or navigation document only one time, throw it in a frame, and then be done with it — not to mention that the frame can stay visible and fixed while other text within the same overall browser window moves.

You can provide more than two frames in a browser window, but that quickly becomes very complex for both you, the author, and your readers. Two or (in extreme cases) three frames are plenty.

Frames do have a few disadvantages to consider. In particular, not all browsers can display them, and not all readers like them. That said, most browsers can display them. If you do them well, your readers can at least tolerate them, and they're quite widespread. Heck, they became popular long before they became part of the HTML 4.0 specification.

Creating a framed site requires planning above all else. First, sit down and sketch out where your frames should go, and give them names. (No, not names like Joey and Sam.) We'd suggest informative names such as "banner" and "body" or "index" and "text." You should also note on your sketch which frame provides the navigation or banner page (and therefore stays constant) and which frame provides the content pages (and therefore changes).

Planning this information now helps you develop content, set up the frames, and set up navigation between the frames.

For the sample site, we want the corporate logo and some navigational links in the top frame, which should take only about 20 percent (about 100 pixels) of the total area of the window. We plan to use the top frame primarily as a navigation tool and let the bottom frame contain the new (changing) content of each link.

After you finish the planning and sketching, you should complete the following steps, each of which is discussed in the following sections:

*1.* Develop content for each frame.

*2.* Develop alternative content for browsers that can't accommodate frames.

*3.* Establish the frameset document.

*4.* Set up the frames.

*5.* Target the frames.

*6.* Test them — extensively.

## *Developing Content*

Developing content for your framed Web site doesn't really pose unique challenges because the content is just a bunch of HTML documents, just like the ones you've done so far.

In fact, if you want to add frames to an existing site, you can still use most of the existing documents with your new frames. If, on the other hand, you're creating a new site, you still must provide content at some point, and this point is as good a time as any.

Start by developing an HTML document, and include content for the navigational or banner page. In the example, we start with the content for the top frame, which is to contain the corporate logo and some navigational links. So far, your HTML document should look just like other HTML documents you've created.

 Because frames that contain corporate logos and navigation links remain visible most of the time, you need to make sure that they look good. You can use any colors and formatting that you'd use in other HTML documents in your framed documents. What's more, you can be very sure that browsers that accommodate frames also accommodate the layout bells and whistles that you like.

Next, you should develop the content for the content pages, creating HTML documents just as you've done so far. In the process, do remember a couple of items about the remaining content pages of your framed site:

✔ **Don't duplicate too much information on your content pages that appears on the navigation or banner page.** If, for example, your top banner — like ours — has the corporate logo, omit that item from the individual pages. And if you include a navigation page, you don't need to include navigation in your content pages.

✔ **Do include some contact and identification information on your content pages.** Readers could possibly access content pages directly, without going through the frames (because the pages are just HTML documents, after all), and if you have no contact or identification information, nobody knows where the pages came from.

Remember the names of your content pages — you need them as you fill in your frames.

# Developing Alternative Content

Because not all browsers accommodate frames (and not all readers choose to display frames), you need to provide alternative content. This alternative content is similar to alternative text you include with images; this text appears in place of images in case your readers can't or choose not to view your images.

***See also*** Part III for more information about alternative text.

In an ideal world, you could take the time to have two complete Web sites — one optimized for nonframed browsers and the other for framed browsers. Realistically, however, you're not likely to have the time for this luxury because having two sites would double the time required to create and maintain them.

Instead, just make a single HTML document that includes all the corporate logos and links that your main frames have and make sure that you include links to all the other pages — the ones that also appear within the frames for the lucky readers. In this alternative content document, you can be as fancy as you want, but keep in mind that browsers that can accommodate cutting-edge formatting can also probably accommodate frames.

# Establishing the Frameset Document

After you develop the content — both for the frames and alternative content — you're ready to set up your *frameset document.* The frameset document tells the browser what frames are available and where they go, in addition to containing some content that only the nonframed browsers can see.

You use the tags listed in the following table to start developing a frameset document.

| HTML Tag or Attribute | Description | Use in Pairs? |
|---|---|---|
| `<FRAMESET>...`<br>`</FRAMESET>` | Establishes frame layout. | Yes |
| `BORDER=n` | Specifies width of border in pixels for all contained frames. | No |
| `BORDERCOLOR=#` | Specifies color for contained rrggbb or name frames. | No |
| `COLS="n,n"` | Specifies column dimensions in pixels, percentage, or in terms of remaining space (`COLS="25%,100,*"`). | No |
| `FRAMEBORDER=n` | Specifies border (1) or no border (0). | No |
| `ROWS="n,n"` | Specifies row dimensions in pixels, percentage, or in terms of remaining space (`ROWS=25%,100,*`). | No |
| `<NOFRAMES>...`<br>`</NOFRAMES>` | Specifies area of frameset document that is visible to frame-incapable browsers. | Yes |

Use the process described in the following steps to set up your frameset document:

*1.* Create a new HTML document, as shown in the following example.

In this document, you do not use `<BODY>` tags; you use `<FRAMESET>` tags instead.

```
<!DOCTYPE HTML PUBLIC "-//W3C//DTD HTML 4.01
   Frameset//EN"
   "http://www.w3.org/TR/html4/frameset.dtd">
<HTML>
<HEAD><TITLE>BLW, Inc.</TITLE></HEAD>
</HTML>
```

*2.* Add a `<FRAMESET>` tag pair, as follows:

```
<!DOCTYPE HTML PUBLIC "-//W3C//DTD HTML 4.01
   Frameset//EN"
   "http://www.w3.org/TR/html4/frameset.dtd">
<HTML>
<HEAD><TITLE>BLW, Inc.</TITLE></HEAD>
<FRAMESET>
</FRAMESET>
</HTML>
```

This example sets up two rows — and no columns — so you need to add a ROWS= attribute to the <FRAMESET> tag. The first (top) row is 100 pixels high, and the remaining row fills the remaining available space, so the complete attribute is ROWS="100,*".

In more complex documents, you can have multiple <FRAME-SET> tags to add frames within frames (such as a set of columns within a set of rows), but that's not necessary in this example.

*3.* Add the ROWS= attribute, as follows:

```
<FRAMESET ROWS="100,*">
</FRAMESET>
```

We could also specify something such as ROWS="25%,*" to make the first row take 25 percent of the window and the second take the rest.

*4.* If you want to remove the frame borders (kind of a neat effect), add the BORDER=0 and FRAMEBORDER=0 attributes to the tag, as follows:

```
<FRAMESET ROWS="100,*" BORDER=0 FRAMEBORDER=0>
</FRAMESET>
```

Why two tags? One for most versions of Netscape Navigator and one for Microsoft Internet Explorer and other HTML 4.0-compliant browsers — dueling browsers require special accommodations.

*5.* Add a <NOFRAMES> tag pair under the <FRAMESET> tag to accommodate browsers that cannot display frames, as shown here:

```
<FRAMESET ROWS="100,*" BORDER=0 FRAMEBORDER=0>
</FRAMESET>
<NOFRAMES>
</NOFRAMES>
```

*6.* Provide regular HTML code within the <NOFRAMES> tags for readers with frame-incapable browsers to see, as the following example shows.

A brief identification and link to the extra content is plenty.

```
<FRAMESET ROWS="100,*" BORDER=0 FRAMEBORDER=0>
</FRAMESET>
<NOFRAMES>
<H1>Welcome to BLW Enterprises!</H1>
<A HREF="noframes.html">Please join us!</A>
</NOFRAMES>
```

A tradition on the Internet is to use this space to berate read-ers for using older browsers. We prefer to assume that the readers are using the browser they choose to use — and which browser they choose is none of our business, so we just wel-come them to the site and send them to the nonframed pages if necessary.

That takes care of establishing the actual structure of the site.

# Setting Up the Frames

Between the <FRAMESET> tags go the <FRAME> tags, which actu-ally build the frames; one frame tag per column or row is called for in the <FRAMESET> tag. So, for this example, we need two <FRAME> tags plus the associated attributes. The following table shows the tags and attributes necessary to create frames.

| HTML Tag or Attribute | Description | Use in Pairs? |
|---|---|---|
| <FRAME> | Establishes frame. | No |
| BORDER=n | Specifies width of border in pixels. | No |
| FRAMEBORDER=n | Specifies border (1) or no border (0). | No |
| NAME="..." | Provides frame name. | No |
| NORESIZE | Prevents reader from resizing frame. | No |
| SCROLLING="..." | Specifies whether the frame can scroll in terms of YES, NO, or AUTO(matic). Yes requires scrollbars; No prohibits them. | No |
| SRC="URL" | Identifies source file that flows into frame. | No |

*Note:* At this point, we assume that you have a complete frameset document and need only to add the <FRAME> tags. The following example builds on the previous one:

```
<!DOCTYPE HTML PUBLIC "-//W3C//DTD HTML 4.01
    Frameset//EN"
    "http://www.w3.org/TR/html4/frameset.dtd">
<HTML>
<HEAD><TITLE>BLW, Inc.</TITLE></HEAD>
<FRAMESET ROWS="100,*" BORDER=0 FRAMEBORDER=0>
</FRAMESET>
<NOFRAMES>
```

```
<H1>Welcome to BLW Enterprises!</H1>
<A HREF="noframes.html">Please join us!</A>
</NOFRAMES>
</HTML>
```

Follow these steps:

**1.** Add the first `<FRAME>` tag, corresponding to the top (banner) frame from the example, as follows:

```
<FRAMESET ROWS="100,*" BORDER=0 FRAMEBORDER=0>
<FRAME>
</FRAMESET>
```

**2.** Add the `SRC=` attribute, which uses a standard URL (absolute or relative) to point to the document that is to fill this frame, as shown in the following example.

This document is one of the documents we developed for our content in a preceding section of this part (specifically in "Developing Content").

```
<FRAME SRC="banner.htm">
```

**3.** Add the `NAME=` attribute to name the frame so that you can refer to it later within HTML documents, as shown here.

We're calling this one "banner" because it acts as a banner at the top of the page.

```
<FRAME SRC="banner.htm" NAME="banner">
```

**4.** Add other attributes, if you want — for example, those that follow.

The `<FRAMESET>` tag turned off the borders, but that can, optionally, also be done in each individual frame. Because the `banner.htm` document is primarily an image of a known size, we turn off the scroll bars and prevent readers from resizing the frame. This setup gives us a little extra layout control but could cause real problems for readers if we accidentally put more content in `banner.htm` than fits in the available space.

```
<FRAME SRC="banner.htm" NAME="banner" NORESIZE
    SCROLLING=NO>
```

**5.** Add the remaining `<FRAME>` tags and attributes, as follows:

```
<FRAME SRC="banner.htm" NAME="banner" NORESIZE
    SCROLLING=NO>
<FRAME SRC="main.htm" NAME="content"
    SCROLLING=AUTO>
```

We choose not to restrict either scrolling or resizing for the content frame; we anticipate that readers probably need to scroll to see all the text and don't want to cause problems. We have no concrete reason to disable those options, so we don't.

Now your frames are complete; so open up your frameset document in your browser and check out the frames. If you've been following this example, you may have frames that appear similar to those shown in the following figure.

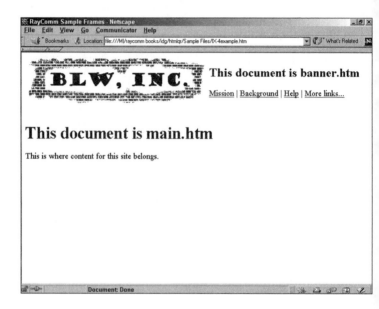

The next step is to make sure that links work correctly and bring up a page in the appropriate window.

# Setting Up Links and Targets

If you've been experimenting with the frames, you may have noticed that some links appear in a completely new window, some appear in the same frame, and some appear in different frames. You, too, can control those links as well. And doing so is easy.

You use an additional attribute, as shown in the following table, for the <A> tag.

| HTML Attribute | Effect | Use in Pairs? |
|---|---|---|
| TARGET="..." | Specifies the default TARGET for links from framed pages. | No |

Each of your links from a framed page should have the additional TARGET= attribute to name the frame in which the link should appear. The previous examples named the top frame "banner" and the lower frame "content" so that links will be targeted accordingly.

To establish a link from the banner.htm document (contained in the banner frame) to the document called mission.htm (which appears within the content frame), add the following TARGET attribute to the existing link:

```
<A HREF="mission.htm" TARGET="content">Mission
    Statement</A>
```

This link opens the Mission Statement (mission.htm) in the content frame, which is the larger frame at the bottom of the browser window. If you omit the target, the link opens in the same frame as the anchor.

Additionally, you have a couple of "magic" target names: _top and _window are the most common and useful. If you target _top, the link replaces your frames in the same window and returns you to a nonframed environment. If you target _window, the link appears in a completely new window. This situation is handy if you're linking to another site or set of documents — your pages remain open while the others are also easily accessible.

Within a Web site, for example, you may suggest that readers access the Dummies home page at www.dummies.com. You probably wouldn't want the Dummies page to appear within one of your frames, however — that'd look silly. You need, therefore, to break out of the frames by using the _window magic target. Your framed site remains open and a new browser window appears with the Dummies home page in it. Just use code such as the following example:

```
<A HREF="http://www.dummies.com/"
    TARGET="_window">Dummies Home Page</A>
```

In addition to working in the <A> tag, the TARGET= attribute works in any other link, such as an imagemap or a form. (The form results appear in the targeted frame.)

# Testing Your Framed Site

After you completely set up your framed site, you want to extensively test the site to make sure that all the pages and links work as you'd hoped. Beyond the obvious step of opening your frameset document in a browser and clicking all the links, a couple of tips may make the process a little easier:

✔ If you edit the frameset document and want to make sure that you reload the changes, click the Location line with the mouse, and then press Enter. If you're sure that you've made and saved frameset document changes, but they don't seem to be appearing in the browser, exit from the browser and open it again.

✔ If you edited one of the documents within a frame and want to reload just that document, click inside the frame, and then click the Reload or Refresh buttons in your browser.

# Developing Style Sheets

In Part X, we step into the realm of HTML 4.01 and Cascading Style Sheets 1 (*a.k.a.,* CSS1).

Style sheets, yet another standard from the World Wide Web Consortium at www.w3.org, provide all of the formatting capabilities and commands you could ever want for your Web pages, and they're the latest hip-hop happening in the HTML world. Style sheets offer a powerful and standard means of formatting your documents, far beyond the relatively limited powers of HTML 4.0 (and 4.01).

If you're just itching to jump into them, be aware that style sheets still have fairly limited and unpredictable browser support. Only Microsoft Internet Explorer 5.0 and 4.0 (and 3.0 to a limited extent) and Netscape Navigator 4.*x* (mostly) support style sheets, and they each provide varying results in displaying style sheet code. Readers who are not using an HTML 4.0-capable browser won't be able to see the nifty formatting effects you add using style sheets. They'll just see a fairly unformatted page with no formatting bells or whistles. We'll give you suggestions about accommodating those wood-burning browsers.

Throughout this part, we assume you're quite familiar with the HTML codes and capabilities from the other parts of this book and have no problem just keying in those codes on command. If you're not quite there yet, brush up on Part I before diving in.

## In this part . . .

About Style Sheets . . . . . . . . . . . . . . . . . . . . . . . . . . 158
Connecting Style Sheets to HTML Documents . . . 160
Developing Style Sheets . . . . . . . . . . . . . . . . . . . . . 164
Gathering a Few Final Tips . . . . . . . . . . . . . . . . . . . 173

# *About Style Sheets*

Style sheets provide formatting commands for Web pages in a more convenient and efficient manner than regular HTML offers. Early versions of HTML offered little or nothing in terms of formatting options; later versions offered formatting capabilities that were associated only with individual occurrences of specific tags. For example, using HTML 3.2 and 4.0 (the most widely supported versions of HTML), you can apply color, size, and font formatting. But to format all of the headings in your document, you had to change the attributes for every heading in your document. Eesch — that's time-consuming!

Now, using style sheets, you can format practically any element of your HTML document and have that formatting applied to the same elements throughout your entire Web site. So, rather than manually changing all those pesky headings, you can simply change the heading style and change the appearance of all of them in one fell swoop.

What else is great about style sheets that isn't also great about plain old HTML? Well, first, there's the fact that you can control formatting more precisely and thoroughly with style sheets than you can with plain HTML. You can control fonts, sizes, colors, alignment, list bullets and numbers, backgrounds (both for the whole document and for individual elements), borders (for any element), and much, much more. Yes, you can do most of these things using plain HTML. Using style sheets, however, you can apply style sheets to entire documents or to specific parts of specified documents — something you can't do with HTML.

Second, the formatting-specific commands from HTML 3.2 are *deprecated* in HTML 4.0 (and 4.01) — which means that they're one step from being as obsolete as an 8-track tape player. And as browsers become more and more 4.0- and 4.01-compliant and more able to use style sheets effectively, there's no guarantee (although it's likely) that they'll continue to support plain old HTML formatting tags to format documents.

Third, as we mentioned, because style sheets can be kept separate from HTML documents, you can make a single style sheet document handle the formatting chores for many different HTML documents. So, when you change that one document, the different formatting will immediately show up in all of the connected documents. If that's not reason enough to dive into style sheets, we don't know what would persuade you.

At the time of writing, browser support for styles sheets is still fairly flaky — er, um, limited and unpredictable. That is, only Microsoft Internet Explorer 5.0 and 4.0 fully support style sheets,

Microsoft Internet Explorer 3.0 provides limited support, and Netscape Navigator 4.0 mostly supports style sheets; however, how each browser displays style sheets varies considerably and may not give you consistent results that you want. Check out www. webreview.com/guides/style/mastergrid.html for a comparative chart showing support for different browsers and different style sheet characteristics.

If you know that your readers are in the roughly 65 percent of the Internet population that uses HTML 4.0 and style sheet-capable browsers, by all means, use style sheets, albeit with some care. If, as is more likely, your readers include some with style sheet-capable browsers and some with older browsers, you have three choices:

- ✔ Use style sheets exclusively and let readers with older browsers see the plain, mostly unformatted text.

- ✔ Use just regular formatting commands from HTML 3.2, with the additional hassle and inconvenience that entails. Pretend that style sheets don't exist.

- ✔ Use both style sheets and regular HTML formatting options. It'll take twice as much effort on your part (and will be redundant and repetitive and format the same thing over and over again) but will accommodate a larger percentage of your readers more effectively than the other options.

Although it's possible to just mix and match style sheets and traditional formatting, that combination will make it fairly difficult to know what formatting commands are specified where and quite difficult to consistently change the formatting. However, this approach makes your documents available and attractive to the largest number of potential readers.

We have found that a good compromise for using style sheets and accommodating browsers that are not HTML 4.0 compliant or that do not reliably handle style sheets is to do the following:

- ✔ Format the background and basic text colors (defined in the <BODY> tag of regular HTML documents) with old-style HTML commands.

- ✔ Format the background and basic text colors with style sheets. (If necessary, these style sheet commands will override the analogous commands from the regular HTML document.)

- ✔ Provide any additional formatting commands through style sheets and, optionally, HTML markup tags.

This process provides some basic formatting for older browsers, yet it still lets you take advantage of the capabilities offered by newer browsers and style sheets. This technique works because of the inheritance of the style sheets.

What's inheritance? *Inheritance* means that the whole document takes on global basic characteristics, and each more specific formatting command that you define overrides the last (for most elements). For example, if you define the background of the whole page as red, the background of a table as blue, and the background of a table cell as green, the most specific formatting (green for the cell) takes precedence.

In general, here's the order of precedence:

- ✔ Document-wide formatting from HTML document (defined in the <BODY> tag) is the most basic.

- ✔ Document-wide formatting from a style sheet overrides document-wide formatting from an HTML document.

- ✔ Specific formatting in HTML overrides document-wide formatting.

- ✔ Specific formatting from a style sheet overrides specific formatting in HTML.

- ✔ Specific formatting from a style sheet overrides general formatting.

In general, if specific formatting is defined in the HTML document and the format for the same element is also defined in a style sheet, the style sheet formatting wins. If a more specific element (such as a table cell, rather than the whole table) is specified either in the style sheet or HTML document, the specific element wins.

Before you get started using style sheets, remember that the style sheet is not necessarily part of the HTML document. In fact, depending on how you do it (we'll tell you the options), the style sheet can be a completely different document. So, the first step is to decide how you want to connect the style sheet to the HTML document. Then you can develop the style sheet, which specifies all the bells and whistles you want to include. We'll show you how to do these steps in the rest of this part.

# *Connecting Style Sheets to HTML Documents*

Your first step in using style sheets is to decide how you want to connect them to your HTML documents. After you get the hang of using style sheets and know how you'll connect them, you might just dive in and start creating them. (You find the exact process later in this part.) For now, however, you need to get an idea of how style sheets and HTML documents can relate.

Basically, style sheets can connect to HTML documents in four ways. You can do any one of the following:

- ✔ Embed the style sheet in the HTML document.

- ✔ Link the style sheet to the HTML document.

- ✔ Import the style sheet into the HTML document.

- ✔ Add style sheet rules as attributes to regular HTML tags.

In this book, we cover only the first two options — mainly because these are the most widely supported options and are the most practical ones to use. (Also, the latter two are somewhat more complicated, convoluted, and out of the scope of the book.) If you're interested in knowing how to use the latter two options, you might check out *HTML 4 For Dummies, 3rd Edition,* by Ed Tittel, Natanya Pitts, and Chelsea Valentine, published by IDG Books Worldwide, Inc.

## Embedding style sheets

The easiest way to handle style sheets is to embed them within the <HEAD> (technically, within <STYLE> tags within the <HEAD>) of the HTML document — easy because you don't have to create a completely different document for the style sheet. You can simply work with an HTML document you already have.

Although embedding style sheets is perhaps the easiest method, it does have one big drawback: The styles apply only to the HTML document that contains it. This means that if you were to make formatting changes to an entire set of HTML documents, you'd have to make changes to each individual HTML document rather than make one change, one time. But, say that you're working with only a single document or perhaps only a few; in such cases, embedding is definitely a good choice.

To embed a style sheet, use the tags and attributes listed in the following table:

| HTML Tag or Attribute | Description | Use in Pairs? |
|---|---|---|
| <STYLE>...</STYLE> | Specifies style block. | Yes |
| TYPE="text/css" | Specifies type of style sheet. | No |
| <!-- --> | Hides style sheet commands from older browsers. | Yes |

The following steps show you how to add the <STYLE> tag and its attributes.

*1.* Start with a functional HTML document. The top of the document should look something like the following example.

```
<!DOCTYPE HTML PUBLIC "-//W3C//DTD HTML 4.01
   Frameset//EN"
   "http://www.w3.org/TR/html4/frameset.dtd">
<HTML>
<HEAD>
<TITLE>Cats Galore</TITLE>
</HEAD>
<BODY>
</BODY>
</HTML>
```

*2.* Add `<STYLE>` tags as shown.

```
<TITLE>Cats Galore</TITLE>
<STYLE>
</STYLE>
</HEAD>
```

*3.* Add comment tags within the `<STYLE>` tags to hide the styles from older browsers.

```
<STYLE>
<!--
-->
</STYLE>
```

*4.* Add the `TYPE="text/css"` attribute to specify that you're using a Cascading Style Sheet. (Other style sheet formats exist, most notably JavaScript Style Sheets, but are less common and nonstandard, so we don't address them in this book.)

```
<STYLE TYPE="text/css">
<!--
-->
</STYLE>
```

That's it! You won't see anything different in the document, but you've found a home for your styles now. When you actually develop the style sheet and specify cool formatting, you add it between the `<STYLE>` tags, as we show you.

## Linking style sheets

Linking style sheets can be a little more confusing than embedding them, mostly because the formatting information is in one location and the actual HTML code is in a completely separate document. That also, however, provides the biggest advantage of style sheets. How? Read on!

Suppose that you have 17 documents in your Web site. You decide you want to add a background image to them all. If you're using embedded style sheets or (horrors!) traditional HTML coding, you'll have to open and edit every one of those 17 documents to add the appropriate code. If, however, you've linked a single style sheet to each of those 17 documents, you need only make a single change in that style sheet and (voilà!) the change happens in each other document. Cool, huh?

You can use the following tags and attributes to link your style sheets:

| HTML Tag or Attribute | Description | Use in Pairs? |
| --- | --- | --- |
| `<LINK>` | Connects document to other information. | No |
| `REL="StyleSheet"` | Specifies that the link is to a style sheet. | No |
| `TYPE="text/css"` | Specifies type of style sheet. | No |
| `HREF="..."` | Indicates URL of linked style sheet. | No |

In linking style sheets, you'll need to create the style sheet file (so that you know the filename to which to link) and include the link within the HTML document.

## Creating the style sheet file

If you've chosen to link to a style sheet, you'll need to create a file that contains the style sheet. The file must be a plain-text file, just like regular HTML documents, and have an extension of .css (instead of .htm or .html). It contains the same style sheet rules you'd use in an embedded style sheet.

## Putting in the link

To link a style sheet to an HTML document, use the following steps:

1. Start with a functional HTML document. The top of the document should look something like the following code:

```
<!DOCTYPE HTML PUBLIC "-//W3C//DTD HTML 4.01
   Frameset//EN"
   "http://www.w3.org/TR/html4/frameset.dtd">
<HTML>
<HEAD>
 <TITLE>Cats Galore</TITLE>
</HEAD>
<BODY>
</BODY>
</HTML>
```

**2.** Add a ⟨LINK⟩ tag, as shown.

```
<TITLE>Cats Galore</TITLE>
<LINK>
</HEAD>
<BODY>
```

**3.** Add the REL="Stylesheet" and TYPE="text/css" attributes to the ⟨LINK⟩ tag.

```
<TITLE>Cats Galore</TITLE>
<LINK REL="StyleSheet" TYPE="text/css">
</HEAD>
```

**4.** Add the HREF"..." attribute to the ⟨LINK⟩ tag.

For the HREF= attribute, simply fill in the name (or address) of the style sheet file.

```
<TITLE>Cats Galore</TITLE>
<LINK REL="StyleSheet" TYPE="text/css"
    HREF="newstyle.css">
</HEAD>
```

That's all there is to linking your document to the newstyle.css style sheet. If the style sheet is in a different folder or on a different server, just adjust the HREF= attribute accordingly — just as you would for any other URL.

You can link and embed a style sheet in the same document. For example, you might have a generic style sheet that applies to most of your HTML documents — that one you'd link. Then, just below the ⟨LINK⟩ tag, you could embed another style sheet with exceptions or additions to the generic style sheet. Both style sheets affect your document, with the style definitions embedded in the document overriding the linked ones.

This capability — to use multiple style sheets — is the cascading part of the Cascading Style Sheet name. You could use a generic style sheet that applies to all of your documents and then a second (or third or fourth) style sheet with formatting specific to the particular document.

# Developing Style Sheets

Developing style sheets differs from most other HTML and Web page creations because the process is more, er, organic. (That's the technical term for trial and error.) Simply because style sheets are fairly new and they don't behave exactly the same on both of the main browsers that support them, you'll find that you must put quite a bit of effort into making small changes in your style sheets and trying them out in different browsers.

To develop a style sheet, you must get the hang of constructing style rules, which are the cryptic pieces of code that make up a style sheet. In the next section, we take a look at how these pieces fit together, and then we show you how to use them to develop a style sheet.

## Constructing style rules

Style sheets are made up of rules, which simply tell browsers how to format HTML elements. Just as HTML tags identify parts of a document — such as a paragraph, heading, table, or list — style rules specify formatting for those elements.

Style rules look a bit different from HTML. For example, instead of using angle brackets as you do with HTML code, you use curly braces ( { } ). And instead of using cryptic-looking abbreviations, you get to use some spelled-out words and descriptions. After you get used to the differences, you might even find style sheets easier to read and work with than HTML code.

*Note:* In this part, we talk about HTML elements but do not use the ⟨ ⟩ because style rules don't use the ⟨ ⟩ symbols. In the actual HTML documents ( but not in the style sheet definitions), you use the HTML tags just as you usually do.

Style rules have two basic parts:

✔ Part that identifies which element the style applies to (techni- cally called the selector)

✔ Part that tells browsers how to display that element (techni- cally called the declaration)

Take a look at an example:

```
P { color: blue }
```

In this example, the P (called the selector) identifies which HTML element the style applies to, and the information within the curly brackets (the property and the value, respectively) tells browsers how to display the element. In this case, the style rule specifies that all paragraphs (P) in the document should be blue.

Also, you can string style rules together, if you find doing so easier. For example, instead of having two separate rules on two lines, like this:

```
P { color: red }
P { background-color: white }
```

you can put the rules together within the same set of brackets by using a semicolon, like this:

```
P { color: red ; background-color: white }
```

You can find all possible properties and values listed in Appendix C.

And, just as you can add multiple declarations and values within the brackets, you can specify multiple elements, like this:

```
H1, H2, H3, H4, H5, H6 { color: green }
```

Notice that when you string elements together, you separate them with commas (not semicolons, as you do between multiple declarations).

One final way to string components together is to stack them, which means to specify a specific element within a more general one. For example, if you want to control the way italics look but only when within a regular paragraph and not anywhere else in the document, you can stack the elements:

```
P I { font-weight: bolder }
```

This style rule specifies that all italic elements that occur within paragraphs should be bolder than normal. Other italics — for example, within headings — would have their normal weight. Notice that stacked elements are not separated by a comma.

With these basic style rule construction concepts in mind, take a look at how to bring it all together.

## Applying style rules

When you decide to use style sheets with your HTML document, you don't need to worry about creating a complete style sheet. It's actually much better to just apply one or two styles at a time, test your results, and then add another rule. Doing too many at once is an overwhelming task and opens the possibility of introducing unexpected problems.

The following table summarizes the various declarations and values we use in the next several sections. *Remember:* Style sheets offer you scads of different capabilities, which you'll find covered in Appendix C.

| *Property* | *Selected Possible Values* |
|---|---|
| font-family | Font names from reader's systems, plus generic choices of serif, sans-serif, or monospace |
| font-size | xx-small, x-small, small, medium, large, x-large, xx-large, smaller, larger |
| font-style | normal, italic, oblique |
| font-variant | normal, small-caps |
| font-weight | normal, bold, bolder, lighter |
| color | **#RRGGBB number** |
| background-color | #RRGGBB **number or color name** |
| background-image | url(. . .) |
| background-attachment | fixed, scroll |
| background-repeat | repeat, repeat-x, repeat-y, no-repeat |
| background-position | %,% |
| float | left, right |

As you can see from this limited sample of declarations and values, the number of style combinations is endless. In general, build style rules one step at a time to keep from getting completely confused:

*1.* Start with an element:

```
<STYLE>
<!--
P
-->
</STYLE>
```

*2.* Add the curly braces:

```
<STYLE>
<!--
P {    }
-->
</STYLE>
```

*3.* Add the property and a colon (space them out for easy reading!):

```
<STYLE>
<!--
P { color:   }
-->
</STYLE>
```

*4.* Add the value, like this:

```
<STYLE>
<!--
P { color: red }
-->
</STYLE>
```

In the rest of this section, we show you a few of the more useful style rules, which should help you get started creating your own style sheet masterpieces. Throughout the remainder of this part, you develop various parts of a style sheet for another of those "cat" documents. For reference purposes, the HTML document used in examples looks like the following illustration before any style sheets are applied.

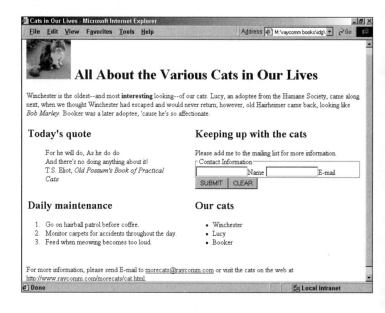

## Setting a font for an entire document

With just a few commands, you can apply formatting to the whole document. To set the font for the entire body (everything within the `<BODY>` and `</BODY>` parts of the HTML document), use the following steps:

*1.* In the style sheet, add the BODY element to specify what the style rule applies to.

```
<STYLE>
<!--
BODY
-->
</STYLE>
```

*2.* Add { and } to contain the style declaration.

```
<STYLE>
<!--
BODY { }
-->
</STYLE>
```

*3.* Add the font-family property, followed by a colon (:).

```
BODY { font-family: }
```

*4.* Add the first choice font.

```
BODY { font-family: Arial }
```

*5.* Add other font choices if you want.

```
BODY { font-family: Arial, Helvetica, Swiss }
```

*6.* Add the closest generic choice from the preceding table.

```
BODY { font-family: Arial, Helvetica,
        Swiss, sans-serif }
```

That's all there is to it. Try it out! We did, with bits and pieces of code from around the book, and came up with something like the following.

## Specifying text and background colors

Another goodie is to specify text and background colors. In the following example, we do this within the same rule.

*Note:* This example builds on the previous one.

1. Add a color style declaration to color the text in the body of the document dark blue.

```
BODY { font-family: Arial, Helvetica,
       Swiss, sans-serif ;
   color: #000066 }
```

2. Add a background-color to set the entire document background to pale yellow.

```
BODY { font-family: Arial, Helvetica,
       Swiss, sans-serif ;
   color: #000066 ;
   background-color: #ffffcc }
```

Note that you can more easily read the styles if each one is on a separate line, as shown here. You're welcome to use spaces or tabs as you need to make the style rule easy to read by humans as well as by computers.

To add other style rules, you need only put more rules on additional lines. Follow these steps:

*Note:* This example builds on the previous one.

1. To color first level headings, you could add an H1 element.

```
BODY { font-family: Arial, Helvetica,
        Swiss, sans-serif ;
      color: 000066 ;
      background-color: ffffcc }
H1 { color: #ff0000 }
```

2. If you want the background of the first level headings — and only of the first level headings — to be white, you can set that, too.

```
BODY { font-family: Arial, Helvetica,
        Swiss, sans-serif ;
      color: #000066 ;
      background-color: #ffffcc }
H1 { color: #ff0000 ;
     background-color: #ffffff }
```

## Specifying background images

You can specify background images for the document as a whole, as you do in HTML, and for individual elements (which you cannot do in HTML). You can also control many aspects of the background image appearance as well. Here's how:

Note: This example builds on the previous one.

1. Add a style declaration to set a background image.

```
BODY { font-family: Arial, Helvetica,
        Swiss, sans-serif ;
      color: #000066 ;
      background-color: #ffffcc ;
      background-image:
      url(winchesterback.jpg) }
```

2. Add another style declaration to keep the image from scrolling so that it looks like a watermark on the screen.

```
BODY { font-family: Arial, Helvetica,
        Swiss, sans-serif ;
      color: #000066 ;
      background-color: #ffffcc ;
      background-image:
      url(winchesterback.jpg) ;
      background-attachment: fixed }
```

*3.* You can also specify the location on the background. We choose 50%, 0% to move it horizontally halfway across the screen, but we leave it all the way at the top.

```
BODY { font-family: Arial, Helvetica,
        Swiss, sans-serif ;
    color: #000066 ;
    background-color: #ffffcc ;
    background-image:
    url(winchesterback.jpg) ;
    background-attachment: fixed ;
    background-position: 50% 0% }
```

*4.* Background-repeat is another particularly handy rule. You can force background images to repeat just horizontally, just vertically, both, or not at all. To preserve the watermark effect, we don't want it to repeat at all in this case.

```
BODY { font-family: Arial, Helvetica,
        Swiss, sans-serif ;
    color: #000066 ;
    background-color: #ffffcc ;
    background-image:
    url(winchesterback.jpg) ;
    background-attachment: fixed ;
    background-position: 50% 0% ;
    background-repeat: no-repeat}
```

## Specifying image alignment

You can use style sheets to control the float of elements — if they go to the left with text flowing around to the right, or vice-versa. This example specifies float for images, but you can also specify float for any block-level elements.

*Note:* This example builds on the previous one.

*1.* Add a style element for IMG.

```
BODY { font-family: Arial, Helvetica,
        Swiss, sans-serif ;
    color: #000066 ;
    background-color: #ffffcc ;
    background-image:
    url(winchesterback.jpg) ;
    background-attachment: fixed ;
    background-position: 50% 0% ;
    background-repeat: no-repeat}
H1 { color: #ff0000 ;
    background-color: #ffffff }
IMG { }
```

2. Add the float declaration, with right as the value.

```
IMG { float: right }
```

That's it! Remember, you follow the same process for adding other cool effects using style sheets.

## Gathering a Few Final Tips

Although no "one right way" exists to develop and format style sheets, some techniques prove more effective than others. Here are a few tips to get you started:

✓ Take care of the document-wide formatting first — that is, specify the background image, background color, and font before you start specifying the nit-picky individual formatting.

✓ Add one or two styles at a time and test them. It's easier to troubleshoot just a few new styles than it is to troubleshoot a whole blob of new ones.

✓ Stay as simple as possible and expand gradually, as you need to. It's easier to add new styles one at a time than it is to backtrack and remove styles.

✓ Remember not to get caught up in the apparent WYSIWYG-ness of style sheets. You still don't have absolute control of the final appearance of the document because your readers might not have style-sheet-capable browsers, might have their browsers set not to use style sheets, or might override your formatting with their own preferred formatting. But they're fun, aren't they?

# HTML Tags

Appendix A provides you with a thorough list of commonly used HTML tags and attributes. Much of the information provided in these tables is discussed in detail in this book; some of the tags and attributes, however, are provided for you to reference as your HTML skills improve and expand. For the latest HTML reference information and specifications, see www.w3.org/.

The tables in Appendix A cover the following:

- ✔ **HTML Structural Markup** — Includes HTML structure tags, document characteristics, tags, and attributes.

- ✔ **HTML Body Markup** — Includes sectional formatting tags that fall within the body.

- ✔ **List Markup** — Includes tags and attributes for creating lists.

- ✔ **Character-level Markup** — Includes HTML tags and attributes used to specify character-level formatting.

- ✔ **Hypertext Anchors and Links Markup** — Includes tags and attributes used to create links and anchors.

- ✔ **Image Markup** — Includes tags and attributes for including images in HTML documents.

- ✔ **Table and Column Markup** — Includes tags and attributes for creating tables.

- ✔ **Form Markup** — Includes tags and attributes for using forms within a document.

- ✔ **Frames and Layers Markup** — Includes tags and attributes for developing frames and layers.

- ✔ **Script Markup** — Includes tags and attributes for using scripts in HTML documents.

- ✔ **Style Sheet Markup** — Includes tags and attributes for using style sheets in HTML documents.

- ✔ **Embedded Applets and Objects** — Includes tag and attributes to include programs or objects within an HTML document.

- ✔ **Internet Explorer Multimedia Extensions** — Includes tags and attributes for adding multimedia to HTML documents. These work with only the Microsoft Internet Explorer (as of press time).

The tables in this appendix are divided into three columns:

- ✔ The *Markup* column provides the specific HTML tag or attribute. Tags are enclosed in pointed brackets; attributes follow the associated tag and in italics. The markup is generally alphabetized by tags, but closely related tags do appear together, regardless of their place in the alphabet. Additionally, tags that are particularly esoteric or not widely accepted are generally located at the end of the tables.

  Additionally, many attributes appear under several different tags. Rather than extensively cross-referencing the attributes, we include them in every place that they apply — the easier to look up the attributes, the better!

- ✔ The *Description* column provides a description of each tag and attribute and minimal guidance about use. In general, characteristics in ALL CAPS are exactly what you may fill in for the ". . ." in the tables. Please refer to the individual Parts of the book for specific instructions. Tags that are not extensively discussed in the book are likely to be fairly similar to other tags — feel free to experiment.

  A ✓ indicates that, at time of publication, approximately 75 percent or more of the browsers in use support the tag. Generally speaking, that means that the most common versions of both Microsoft Internet Explorer and Netscape Navigator support the tag. Using checked tags, however, could still exclude up to 25 percent of your potential audience.

- ✔ The *Reference or Usage* column provides information about the HTML versions (or specific browsers) that support the tag or attribute.

  An ✓ indicates that the tag is *deprecated* (strongly discouraged) in HTML 4.0 and will likely be rendered obsolete in the next version of HTML. You may need to use some of these deprecated tags to meet the needs of your audience now, but if your audience will be using very new browsers that support style sheets and HTML 4.0 completely, we strongly suggest that you avoid deprecated elements.

  ***Note:*** Most deprecated elements are formatting-specific elements that offer capabilities better accomplished through style sheets.

  Tags and attributes included in Netscape Navigatorand Internet Explorer (labeled Navigator/IE, or IE/Navigator, depending on the better support) work only if the reader is using those specific browser packages. If a tag is available only in Navigator or Internet Explorer, be advised that it may never gain wider acceptance.

*Table A-1*   *Structural Markup*

| Markup | Description | Reference or Usage |
|---|---|---|
| `<!DOCTYPE HTML PUBLIC "-//W3C//DTD HTML.4.0 Final//EN">` | ✓Identifies document as conforming to the HTML specification. Required at top of all HTML documents. Mandatory in HTML 4.0. | HTML 2.0 |
| `<HTML>. . . </HTML>` | ✓Encloses the entire document and identifies it as HTML. | HTML 2.0 |
| `<HEAD>. . . </HEAD>` | ✓Sets off the document header information, including the title. | HTML 2.0 |
| `<TITLE>. . . </TITLE>` | ✓Encloses the document title. Mandatory in HTML 3.2 and 4.0. | HTML 2.0 |
| `<BASE>` | ✓Specifies general document link information about the current file so that links and relative URLs are interpreted correctly. Use only if necessary in your specific application. | HTML 2.0 |
| `HREF="URL"` | ✓Specifies the URL of current file so that relative URLs are interpreted correctly. | HTML 2.0 |
| `TARGET=". . ."` | ✓Specifies the default target for links from framed pages. | HTML 4.0 |
| `<LINK>` | Specifies the general relationships of the current document to other documents. | HTML 2.0 |
| `REV=MADE HREF="URL"` | Identifies author or URL. Other link attributes exist but are seldom used or recognized by browsers. | HTML 2.0 |
| `REL=STYLESHEET TYPE= "text/css" HREF="URL"` | Links CSS1 Stylesheet. | HTML 4.0 |

cont.

*Table A-1 (continued)*

| Markup | Description | Reference or Usage |
|---|---|---|
| `<META . . . >` | ✓Provides information about the document attributes. Could include `CONTENT=`, `NAME=` and `HTTP-EQUIV=` attributes. | HTML 2.0 |
| `<META NAME="KEYWORDS" CONTENT=". . .">` | ✓Identifies document keywords for use by search and indexing services. | HTML 2.0 |
| `<META NAME= "DESCRIPTION" CONTENT=". . .">` | ✓Identifies document summary for use by search and indexing services. | HTML 2.0 |
| `<META HTTP-EQUIV= "Refresh" Content = "n;URL=...">` | ✓Automatically changes to page specified by `URL=` after number of seconds specified by `n`. | HTML 2.0 |
| `<BODY>. . . </BODY>` | ✓Identifies all information included in the main portion (body) of the document. | HTML 2.0 |
| `ALINK="#rrggbb"` or `"name"` | ✓Colors the links in your document based on the `rrggbb` number or the standard color name. `ALINK` stands for the active link. | HTML 3.2 ✗ |
| `BACKGROUND="URL"` | ✓Places an image behind the text in your HTML document. | HTML 3.2 ✗ |
| `BGCOLOR="#rrggbb"` or `"name"` | ✓Colors the background based on the `rrggbb` number or the standard color name. | HTML 3.2 ✗ |
| `BGPROPERTIES=fixed` | Specifies a nonscrolling background image. | IE |
| `LEFTMARGIN=n` | Specifies the left margin for the entire body of the page in pixels. | IE |
| `LINK="#rrggbb"` or `"name"` | ✓Colors the links in your document based on the `rrggbb` number or the standard color name. `LINK` is for the anchor text visible in the document. | HTML 3.2 ✗ |

| Markup | Description | Reference or Usage |
|---|---|---|
| *TEXT="#rrggbb"* or *"name"* | ✓Colors all the normal text in the document based on the rrggbb number or the standard color name. | HTML 3.2 ✗ |
| *TOPMARGIN=n* | Specifies the margin for the top of the page in pixels. | IE |
| *VLINK="#rrggbb"* or *"name"* | ✓Colors the visited links in your document based on the rrggbb number or the standard color name. VLINK stands for visited link. | HTML 3.2 ✗ |

*Table A-2    Body Markup*

| Markup | Description | Reference or Usage |
|---|---|---|
| `<!--...-->` | ✓Provides a place to insert comments. Comments are ignored by the browser yet visible in the source. | HTML 2.0 |
| `<ADDRESS>...` `</ADDRESS>` | ✓Encloses information about the author and the document. | HTML 2.0 |
| `<BLOCKQUOTE>...` `</BLOCKQUOTE>` | ✓Encloses a quotation. | HTML 2.0 |
| `<BR>` | ✓Forces a line break. | HTML 2.0 |
| *CLEAR="..."* | ✓Forces clear margins (below images or objects) on the LEFT, RIGHT, or BOTH. | HTML 3.2 |
| `<DIV>...</DIV>` | ✓Indicates a division or section within a document. | HTML 2.0 |
| *ALIGN="..."* | ✓Aligns the division (or section) to the LEFT, RIGHT, or CENTER. The deprecated tags `<CENTER>. . .</CENTER>` are nonstandard abbreviations of `<DIV ALIGN=CENTER>. . .</DIV>`. | HTML 3.2 |
| *LANG="..."* | Indicates ISO languages used in section. | HTML 4.0 |

**cont.**

*Table A-2 (continued)*

| Markup | Description | Reference or Usage |
|---|---|---|
| NOWRAP | Prevents text wrap within the section. | IE |
| ⟨H1⟩...⟨/H1⟩<br>⟨H2⟩...⟨/H2⟩<br>⟨H3⟩...⟨/H3⟩<br>⟨H4⟩...⟨/H4⟩<br>⟨H5⟩...⟨/H5⟩<br>⟨H6⟩...⟨/H6⟩ | ✓Indicate headings ranging from ⟨H1⟩ to ⟨H6⟩ (the least important). The ⟨H1⟩ tags are normally used for the document title or main heading. | HTML 2.0 |
| *ALIGN="..."* | ✓Aligns the heading to the LEFT, RIGHT, or CENTER. | HTML 3.2 ✗ |
| *NOBR* | Prevents text breaks or line wraps within tag. | Navigator |
| ⟨HR⟩ | ✓Specifies a horizontal rule. | HTML 3.2 |
| *ALIGN="..."* | ✓Specifies whether the horizontal rule should be at the LEFT, RIGHT, or CENTER. | HTML 3.2 ✗ |
| *NOSHADE* | ✓Prohibits horizontal rule shading. | HTML 3.2 |
| *SIZE=n* | ✓Indicates the height (in pixels of the horizontal rule. | HTML 3.2 ✗ |
| *WIDTH="n"* | ✓Specifies an exact width of the horizontal rule in pixels or a relative width measured as a percentage of document width. | HTML 3.2 ✗ |
| ⟨NOBR⟩...<br>⟨/NOBR⟩ | Specifies a string of elements without line breaks. | Navigator |
| ⟨P⟩...⟨/P⟩ | ✓Indicates the beginning of a paragraph (the closing ⟨/P⟩ tag is optional). | HTML 2.0 |
| *ALIGN="..."* | ✓Aligns the paragraph to the LEFT, RIGHT, or CENTER. | HTML 3.2 |
| ⟨PRE⟩...<br>⟨/PRE⟩ | ✓Encloses blocks of text to be shown verbatim in a fixed-width font (white space and line breaks are significant). | HTML 2.0 |
| *WIDTH=n* | ✓Specifies a width for the section in characters. | HTML 3.2 |
| ⟨WBR⟩ | Identifies where a line break can be inserted by the browser, if necessary, within a ⟨NOBR⟩ section. | Navigator |

*Table A-3*    *List Markup*

| Markup | Description | Reference or Usage |
|---|---|---|
| ⟨DL⟩...<br>⟨/DL⟩ | ✓Provides a definition list. | HTML 2.0 |
| ⟨DT⟩ | ✓Begins each item title in the definition list. | HTML 2.0 |
| ⟨DD⟩ | ✓Begins each item definition in the definition list. | HTML 2.0 |
| ⟨LI⟩ | ✓Identifies each item in a ⟨DIR⟩, ⟨MENU⟩, ⟨OL⟩, or ⟨UL⟩ list. | HTML 2.0 |
| *TYPE=A, a,*<br>*I, i, 1,* or<br>*CIRCLE, SQUARE,*<br>or *DISC* | ✓Specifies the style of a list item. A= large letters; a= small letters; I= large Roman numerals; i= small Roman numerals; 1= numbers. | HTML 3.2 *✗* |
| *VALUE=n* | ✓Changes the count of ordered lists as they progress. | HTML 3.2 |
| ⟨OL⟩...⟨/OL⟩ | ✓Specifies ordered (numbered) lists. | HTML 2.0 |
| *START=n* | ✓Specifies a starting number for the list. | HTML 3.2 |
| *TYPE=A, a,*<br>*I, i,* or *1* | ✓Specifies the style of an ordered list. A= large letters; a= small letters; I= large Roman numerals; i= small Roman numerals; 1= numbers. | HTML 3.2 *✗* |
| ⟨UL⟩...<br>⟨/UL⟩ | ✓Encloses unordered lists. | HTML 2.0 |
| *TYPE=SQUARE,*<br>*CIRCLE, DISC* | ✓Specifies the style of an unordered list. | HTML 3.2 *✗* |

*Table A-4*    *Character-Level Markup*

| Markup | Description | Reference or Usage |
|---|---|---|
| ⟨ACRONYM⟩...<br>⟨/ACRONYM⟩ | Identifies acronyms. | HTML 4.0 |
| *TITLE="..."* | Provides full text of acronym. | HTML 4.0 |
| ⟨B⟩...⟨/B⟩ | ✓Makes text bold. | HTML 2.0 |
| ⟨BASEFONT⟩ | ✓Specifies font information for the document. | HTML 3.2 *✗* |

cont.

*Table A-4 (continued)*

| Markup | Description | Reference or Usage |
|---|---|---|
| `COLOR="#rrggbb"` or `"name"` | ✓Colors the text based on the rrggbb number or the standard color name. | IE/Navigator ✗ |
| `FACE="..."` | ✓Sets the typeface name. A list of font names can be specified. | IE/Navigator ✗ |
| `SIZE=n` | ✓Changes the size n, on a scale from 1 to 7, of the base font, which also changes the size of fonts that are based on the base font. | HTML 3.2 ✗ |
| `<BIG>...</BIG>` | ✓Makes text big. | HTML 3.2 |
| `<BLINK>...</BLINK>` | Makes text blink. | Navigator |
| `<CITE>...</CITE>` | ✓Marks a citation of a book, article, movie, and so on and is often displayed in italics. | HTML 2.0 |
| `<CODE>...</CODE>` | ✓Marks a piece of computer source code and is often displayed in a fixed-width font. | HTML 2.0 |
| `<DEL>...</DEL>` | Indicates deleted text. | HTML 4.0 |
| `CITE="url"` | Indicates reference source for deletion. | HTML 4.0 |
| `<DFN>...</DFN>` | Marks defining (first) occurrence of term. | HTML 3.2 |
| `<EM>...</EM>` | ✓Emphasizes text, usually HTML, by displaying it as italics. | HTML 2.0 |
| `<FONT>...</FONT>` | ✓Specifies the font. | HTML 3.2 ✗ |
| `COLOR="#rrggbb"` or `"name"` | ✓Colors the text based on the rrggbb number or the standard color name. | HTML 3.2 ✗ |
| `FACE="..."` | ✓Sets the typeface name. A list of font names can be specified. | IE/Navigator ✗ |
| `SIZE="n"` | ✓Changes the font size on a scale from 1 to 7. | HTML 3.2 ✗ |
| `<I>...</I>` | ✓Makes text italic. | HTML 2.0 |

| Markup | Description | Reference or Usage |
|--------|-------------|--------------------|
| `<INS>...`<br>`</INS>` | Indicates inserted text. | HTML 4.0 |
| `CITE="url"` | Indicates reference source for deletion. | HTML 4.0 |
| `<KBD>...`<br>`</KBD>` | ✓Shows an example of a keyboard entry or user input. | HTML 2.0 |
| `<S>...</S>`<br>or `<STRIKE>...`<br>`</STRIKE>` | ✓Overstrikes text. | HTML 2.0 ✗ |
| `<SAMP>...`<br>`</SAMP>` | ✓Shows literal characters, such as computer output. | HTML 2.0 |
| `<SMALL>...`<br>`</SMALL>` | ✓Makes text small. | HTML 3.2 |
| `<STRONG>...`<br>`</STRONG>` | ✓Gives strong emphasis to text. Often displayed as bold. | HTML 2.0 |
| `<SUB>...`<br>`</SUB>` | ✓Makes text subscript. | HTML 2.0 |
| `<SUP>...`<br>`</SUP>` | ✓Makes text superscript. | HTML 2.0 |
| `<TT>...`<br>`</TT>` | ✓Creates typewriter (fixed-width) font. | HTML 2.0 |
| `<U>...</U>` | ✓Underlines text. | HTML 2.0 ✗ |
| `<VAR>...`<br>`</VAR>` | ✓Shows the name of a variable. Often displayed as italic. | HTML 2.0 |

*Table A-5*    *Hypertext Anchors/Links Markup*

| Markup | Description | Reference or Usage |
|--------|-------------|--------------------|
| `<A>...</A>` | ✓Marks an anchor. | HTML 2.0 |
| `ACCESSKEY=`<br>`"..."` | Indicates the key to bring focus to the field. | HTML 4.0 |
| `HREF="URL"` | ✓Creates a link to the specified URL. | HTML 2.0 |
| `NAME="..."` | ✓Creates a named anchor. | HTML 2.0 |
| `TARGET="..."` | ✓Specifies the default `TARGET` for links from framed pages. | HTML 4.0 |

cont.

*Table A-5 (continued)*

| Markup | Description | Reference or Usage |
|---|---|---|
| *TABINDEX=n* | Indicates the numeric location of the tab position within the document. | HTML 4.0 |
| *TITLE="..."* | ✓Identifies title or label for anchor. | HTML 3.2 |

*Table A-6    Image Markup*

| Markup | Description | Reference or Usage |
|---|---|---|
| `<IMG>` | ✓Inserts an image. | HTML 2.0 |
| *SRC="URL"* | ✓Specified URL of image to include. | HTML 2.0 |
| *ALIGN="..."* | ✓Places the object within the page. RIGHT and LEFT float the object as specified and wrap text around it. MIDDLE, TOP, and BOTTOM align relative to surrounding text. | HTML 3.2 ✗ |
| *ALT="..."* | ✓Specifies the text that should appear if the image does not. | HTML 2.0 |
| *BORDER=n* | ✓Controls the thickness of the border around an image in pixels. | HTML 3.2 |
| *HEIGHT=n* | ✓Specifies the height of the image in pixels. | HTML 3.2 |
| *HSPACE=n* | ✓Controls the horizontal space (white space) around the image in pixels. | HTML 3.2 |
| *ISMAP* | ✓Specifies that the image is a server-side clickable imagemap. | HTML 2.0 |
| *LOWSRC="URL"* | Specifies a low resolution image that will load first and then be replaced by the SRC image. | Navigator |
| *TITLE="..."* | ✓Specifies title to appear with image. | HTML 4.0 |
| *USEMAP="mapname"* | ✓Identifies the picture as a client-side imagemap and specifies a MAP to use for acting on the user's clicks. | HTML 3.2 |
| *VSPACE=n* | ✓Controls the vertical space (white space) around the image in pixels. | HTML 3.2 |
| *WIDTH=n* | ✓Specifies the width of the image in pixels. | HTML 3.2 |
| `<MAP>` | ✓Specifies a collection of hot spots for a client-side imagemap. | HTML 3.2 |

| Markup | Description | Reference or Usage |
|---|---|---|
| `NAME="..."` | ✓Gives the MAP a name so it can be referred to later. | HTML 3.2 |
| `<AREA>` | ✓Specifies the shape of a "hot spot" in a client-side imagemap. | HTML 3.2 |
| `ALT="..."` | ✓Specifies the text associated with the link. | HTML 3.2 |
| `COORDS="x1, y1, x2, y2, ..."` | ✓Specifies coordinates that define the hot spot's shape. | HTML 3.2 |
| `HREF="URL"` | ✓Specifies the destination of the hot spot. See above. | HTML 3.2 |
| `NOHREF` | ✓Indicates that clicks in this region should cause no action. | HTML 3.2 |
| `SHAPE="..."` | ✓Specifies type of shape as RECT (rectangle), CIRCLE, or POLYGON. | HTML 3.2 |
| `TARGET="..."` | ✓Specifies the default TARGET for links from framed pages. | HTML 4.0 |
| `TABINDEX=n` | Specifies sequence number for readers who use the tab key to maneuver around the page. | HTML 4.0 |

*Table A-7    Table and Column Markup*

| Markup | Description | Reference or Usage |
|---|---|---|
| `<TABLE>...` `</TABLE>` | ✓Creates a table. | HTML 3.2 |
| `ALIGN="..."` | ✓Aligns the text to the LEFT, RIGHT, CENTER. | HTML 3.2 ✗ |
| `BACKGROUND= "URL"` | Specifies background image for the table. | IE ✗ |
| `BGCOLOR= "#rrggbb"` or `"name"` | ✓Sets background color by rrggbb number or standard color name. | Navigator/IE ✗ |
| `BORDER=n` | ✓Draws borders around table cells. The number determines the size in pixels. | HTML 3.2 ✗ |

**cont.**

*Table A-7 (continued)*

| Markup | Description | Reference or Usage |
|---|---|---|
| *BORDERCOLOR= "#rrggbb"* or *"name"* | Specifies border color by rrggbb number or standard color name and must be used with the BORDER attribute. | IE ✗ |
| *BORDERCOLOR DARK="#rrggbb"* or *"name"* | Sets independent border color control by rrggbb number or standard color name for one of the two colors used to draw a 3-D border. Must be used with the BORDER attribute. | IE ✗ |
| *BORDERCOLOR LIGHT="#rrggbb"* or *"name"* | Sets independent border color control by rrggbb number or standard color name for one of the two colors used to draw a 3-D border. Must be used with the BORDER attribute. | IE ✗ |
| *CELLPADDING=n* | ✓Inserts space between the cell border and the cell contents. The number determines the size in pixels. | HTML 3.2 |
| *CELLSPACING=n* | ✓Inserts specified space between cells. The number determines the size in pixels. | HTML 3.2 |
| *CLEAR="..."* | ✓Specifies where text following table begins as NO (text follows table immediately), LEFT (starts as left-aligned line), RIGHT (right-aligned line), ALL (first blank line after table). | IE/Navigator |
| *COLS=n* | Sets the number of columns in table. | IE/Navigator ✗ |
| *FRAME="..."* | Specifies outer border for the table as BORDER, VOID, ABOVE, BELOW, HSIDES (horizontal sides), LHS (left hand side), RHS (right hand side), VSIDES (vertical sides), BOX. | IE ✗ |
| *NOWRAP* | Keeps table rows from wrapping if they go past the right margin. | IE/Navigator |
| *RULES="..."* | Specifies inner borders for table as GROUPS (based on IE specific table tags COLGROUP, THEAD, TBODY, TFOOT), ROWS, COLS, or ALL. | IE ✗ |
| *WIDTH=n* | ✓Describes the table width in terms of the number of pixels or the percentage of the document width. | HTML 3.2 ✗ |

| Markup | Description | Reference or Usage |
|---|---|---|
| `<CAPTION>...`<br>`</CAPTION>` | ✓Identifies table caption. | HTML 3.2 |
| `ALIGN="..."` | Aligns the text to the `LEFT`, `RIGHT`, `TOP`, or `BOTTOM` | HTML 3.2 |
| `<TR>...</TR>` | ✓Inserts table row. | HTML 3.2 |
| `ALIGN="..."` | ✓Aligns the text to the `LEFT`, `RIGHT`, `CENTER`, `JUSTIFY`, or `CHAR`. CHAR aligns on the decimal point or on character specified by `CHAR="..."`. | HTML 3.2 |
| `BGCOLOR=`<br>`"#rrggbb"`<br>or `"name"` | ✓Sets background color by `rrggbb` number or standard color name. | Navigator/IE ✗ |
| `BORDERCOLOR=`<br>`"#rrggbb"`<br>or `"name"` | Specifies border color by `rrggbb` number or standard color name and must be used with the `BORDER` attribute. | IE ✗ |
| `NOWRAP` | ✓Keeps table row from wrapping when they go past the right margin. | IE |
| `VALIGN="..."` | ✓Aligns the text to the `TOP`, `MIDDLE`, or `BOTTOM`. | HTML 3.2 |
| `<TD>...</TD>` | ✓Specifies a standard table data cell. | HTML 3.2 |
| `ALIGN="..."` | ✓Aligns the text to the `LEFT`, `RIGHT`, `CENTER`, `JUSTIFY`, or `CHAR`. CHAR aligns on the decimal point or on character specified by `CHAR="..."`. | HTML 3.2 |
| `BACKGROUND=`<br>`"..."` | Specifies background image. | IE ✗ |
| `BGCOLOR=`<br>`"#rrggbb"`<br>or `"name"` | ✓Sets background color by `rrggbb` number or standard color name. | Navigator/IE ✗ |
| `BORDERCOLOR=`<br>`"#rrggbb"`<br>or `"name"` | Specifies border color by `rrggbb` number or standard color name and must be used with the `BORDER` attribute. | IE ✗ |
| `COLSPAN=n` | ✓Specifies how many columns of the table this cell should span. | HTML 3.2 |
| `HEIGHT="n"` | ✓Describes the cell height in terms of the number of pixels. | HTML 3.2 ✗ |

cont.

*Table A-7 (continued)*

| Markup | Description | Reference or Usage |
|---|---|---|
| NOWRAP | ✓Indicates that the lines within this cell cannot be broken to fit in the cell. | HTML 3.2 |
| ROWSPAN=n | ✓Specifies how many rows of the table this cell should span. | HTML 3.2 |
| VALIGN="..." | ✓Controls vertical alignment within the cell. Values are TOP, MIDDLE, BOTTOM. | HTML 3.2 |
| WIDTH="n" | ✓Describes the cell width in terms of the number of pixels or the percentage of the table width. | HTML 3.2 ✗ |
| &lt;TH&gt;...&lt;/TH&gt; | ✓Specifies a table header. | HTML 3.2 |
| ALIGN="..." | ✓Aligns the text to the LEFT, RIGHT, CENTER, JUSTIFY, or CHAR. CHAR aligns on the decimal point or on character specified by CHAR="...". | HTML 3.2 |
| BACKGROUND= "URL" | Specifies background image for the cell. | IE ✗ |
| BGCOLOR= "#rrggbb" or "name" | ✓Sets background color by rrggbb number or standard color name. | Navigator/IE ✗ |
| BORDERCOLOR= "#rrggbb" or "name" | Specifies border color by rrggbb number or standard color name and must be used with the BORDER attribute. | IE ✗ |
| COLSPAN=n | ✓Specifies how many columns of the table this cell should span. | HTML 3.2 |
| HEIGHT="n" | ✓Describes the cell height in terms of the number of pixels. | HTML 3.2 ✗ |
| NOWRAP | ✓Indicates that the lines within this cell cannot be broken to fit in the cell. | HTML 3.2 |
| ROWSPAN=n | ✓Specifies how many rows of the table this cell should span. | HTML 3.2 |
| VALIGN="..." | ✓Controls vertical alignment within the cell. Values are TOP, MIDDLE, BOTTOM. | HTML 3.2 |
| WIDTH="n" | ✓Describes the cell width in terms of the number of pixels, or the percentage of the table width. | HTML 3.2 ✗ |

| *Markup* | *Description* | *Reference or Usage* |
|---|---|---|
| `<THEAD>`... `</THEAD>` | Defines table heading section. | HTML 4.0 |
| `ALIGN="..."` | Aligns the text to the `LEFT`, `RIGHT`, `CENTER`, `JUSTIFY`, or `CHAR`. CHAR aligns on the decimal point or on character specified by `CHAR="..."`. | HTML 4.0 |
| `VALIGN="..."` | Controls vertical alignment within the cell range. Values are `TOP`, `MIDDLE`, `BOTTOM`. | HTML 4.0 |
| `<TBODY>`... `</TBODY>` | Marks body of table. | HTML 4.0 |
| `ALIGN="..."` | Aligns the text to the `LEFT`, `RIGHT`, `CENTER`, `JUSTIFY`, or `CHAR`. CHAR aligns on the decimal point or on character specified by `CHAR="..."`. | HTML 4.0 |
| `VALIGN="..."` | Controls vertical alignment within the cell range. Values are `TOP`, `MIDDLE`, `BOTTOM`. | HTML 4.0 |
| `<TFOOT>`... `</TFOOT>` | Defines table footer section. | HTML 4.0 |
| `ALIGN="..."` | ✓Aligns the text to the `LEFT`, `RIGHT`, `CENTER`, `JUSTIFY`, or `CHAR`. CHAR aligns on the decimal point or on character specified by `CHAR="..."`. | HTML 4.0 |
| `VALIGN="..."` | Controls vertical alignment within the cell range. Values are `TOP`, `MIDDLE`, `BOTTOM`. | HTML 4.0 |
| `<COLGROUP>`... `</COLGROUP>` | Sets properties for columns within tables. | HTML 4.0 |
| `ALIGN="..."` | Aligns the text to the `LEFT`, `RIGHT`, `CENTER`, `JUSTIFY`, or `CHAR`. CHAR aligns on the decimal point or on character specified by `CHAR="..."`. | HTML 4.0 |
| `SPAN=n` | Specifies number of contiguous columns in group to which properties should apply. | HTML 4.0 |
| `VALIGN="..."` | Controls vertical alignment within the cell. Values are `TOP`, `MIDDLE`, `BOTTOM`. | HTML 4.0 |
| `WIDTH="n"` | Indicates width of columns in group. | HTML 4.0 |

*Note:* To implement forms, you must be using an HTTP server that supports those options. Check with your server administrator for the complete details.

*Table A-8    Form Markup*

| Markup | Description | Reference or Usage |
|---|---|---|
| `<FORM ...>` `... </FORM>` | ✓Encloses the entire form. | HTML 2.0 |
| `ACTION="..."` | ✓Identifies what program processes the data when the form is submitted to a gateway program. | HTML 2.0 |
| `ENCTYPE="..."` | Identifies `MIME` type of form data. | HTML 2.0 |
| `METHOD="..."` | ✓Identifies method for submitting form. Valid options are `GET` or `POST`, and one or the other is required. | HTML 2.0 |
| `TARGET="..."` | ✓Specifies the target frame for the forms to appear in if you're using framed pages. | HTML 4.0 |
| `onSubmit= "..."` | ✓Calls script (JavaScript or VBScript) event when form is submitted. | HTML 4.0 |
| `<INPUT...>` | ✓Identifies an input field. | HTML 2.0 |
| `CHECKED` | ✓Shows which item is selected by default (check boxes/radio buttons). | HTML 2.0 |
| `MAXLENGTH=n` | ✓Indicates the maximum number of characters in the field. | HTML 2.0 |
| `NAME="..."` | ✓Indicates the name of the field. | HTML 2.0 |
| `ID="..."` | Indicates a unique ID for the field. | HTML 4.0 |
| `SIZE=n` | ✓Displays a field n characters wide. | HTML 2.0 |
| `SRC="URL"` | ✓Specifies URL address of image to be used if `TYPE=IMAGE`. | HTML 3.2 |
| `TYPE="..."` | ✓Indicates the type of field. Valid types are `TEXT`, `PASSWORD`, `CHECKBOX`, `RADIO`, `SUBMIT`, `RESET`, `IMAGE`, `HIDDEN`, `FILE`, `BUTTON`, and `IMAGE`. | HTML 2.0 |
| `VALUE="..."` | ✓Indicates the value of the input field (the label for Submit and Reset buttons). | HTML 2.0 |
| `TITLE="..."` | Specifies extra information to appear with field. | HTML 4.0 |

| *Markup* | *Description* | *Reference or Usage* |
|---|---|---|
| *ACCESSKEY=* *"..."* | Indicates the key used to bring focus to the field. | HTML 4.0 |
| *DISABLED* | Disables the field. | HTML 4.0 |
| *TABINDEX=n* | Indicates the numeric location of the tab position within the document. | HTML 4.0 |
| *onBlur="..."* | ✓Calls script (JavaScript or VBScript) event if reader moves out of field. | HTML 4.0 |
| *onChange=* *"..."* | ✓Calls script (JavaScript or VBScript) event if user changes field. | HTML 4.0 |
| *onClick=* *"..."* | ✓Calls script (JavaScript or VBScript) event if user clicks in field. | HTML 4.0 |
| *onFocus=* *"..."* | ✓Calls script (JavaScript or VBScript) event if user moves into field. | HTML 4.0 |
| *onSelect=* *"..."* | ✓Calls script (JavaScript or VBScript) event if user selects field. | HTML 4.0 |
| <SELECT...> ... </SELECT> | ✓Provides a list of items to select. | HTML 2.0 |
| *MULTIPLE* | ✓Indicates that multiple selections are allowed. | HTML 2.0 |
| *NAME="..."* | ✓Indicates the name of the field. | HTML 2.0 |
| *SIZE=n* | ✓Determines the size of the scrollable list by showing n options. | HTML 2.0 |
| *ID="..."* | Indicates a unique ID for the field. | HTML 4.0 |
| *ACCESSKEY=* *"..."* | Indicates the key to bring focus to the field. | HTML 4.0 |
| *DISABLED* | Disables the field. | HTML 4.0 |
| *TABINDEX=n* | Indicates the numeric location of the tab position within the document. | HTML 4.0 |
| <OPTION...> | ✓Precedes each item in an option list. The closing </OPTION> tag is optional. | HTML 2.0 |
| *SELECTED* | ✓Identifies which option is selected by default. | HTML 2.0 |
| *VALUE="..."* | ✓Indicates value of the field. | HTML 2.0 |
| <TEXTAREA...> ... </TEXTAREA> | ✓Encloses a multiline text field. The enclosed text is the value appearing in the field. | HTML 2.0 |

**cont.**

*Table A-8 (continued)*

| Markup | Description | Reference or Usage |
|---|---|---|
| `ID="..."` | Indicates a unique ID for the field. | HTML 4.0 |
| `COLS=n` | ✓Indicates the number of columns in the field. | HTML 2.0 |
| `NAME="..."` | ✓Indicates the name of the field. | HTML 2.0 |
| `ROWS=n` | ✓Indicates the number of rows in the field. | HTML 2.0 |
| `ACCESSKEY="..."` | Indicates the key to bring focus to the field. | HTML 4.0 |
| `DISABLED` | Disables the field. | HTML 4.0 |
| `TABINDEX=n` | Indicates the numeric location of the tab position within the document. | HTML 4.0 |
| `<BUTTON...> ... </BUTTON>` | Places button in form to activate scripts or submit form. | HTML 4.0 |
| `NAME="..."` | Indicates the name of the field. | HTML 4.0 |
| `TYPE="..."` | Indicates the type of button. Valid types are `BUTTON`, `SUBMIT`, and `RESET`. | HTML 4.0 |
| `VALUE="..."` | Indicates the value of the input field (the label for Submit and Reset buttons). | HTML 4.0 |
| `DISABLED` | Indicates the name of the field. | HTML 4.0 |
| `TABINDEX=n` | Indicates the numeric location of the tab position within the document. | HTML 4.0 |
| `ACCESSKEY="..."` | Indicates the key to bring focus to the field. | HTML 4.0 |
| `<LABEL...> ... </LABEL>` | Specifies label for form input control. | HTML 4.0 |
| `FOR="..."` | Indicates the ID of the field the label applies to. | HTML 4.0 |
| `<FIELDSET> ... </FIELDSET>` | Encloses a logical set of form fields for easier access. | HTML 4.0 |
| `<LEGEND>... </LEGEND>` | Specifies label for fieldset. | HTML 4.0 |
| `ALIGN="..."` | Aligns the legend to the `LEFT`, `RIGHT`, `TOP` or `BOTTOM`. | HTML 4.0 |

*Table A-9*    *Frames and Layers*

| Markup | Description | Reference or Usage |
|---|---|---|
| `<FRAME>` | ✓Establishes a frame. | HTML 4.0 |
| `BORDER=n` | Specifies width of border in pixels. | Frames (Navigator) |
| `FRAMEBORDER=n` | ✓Specifies border (1) or no border (0). | HTML 4.0 |
| `MARGINHEIGHT=n` | ✓Specifies margin height for frame in pixels. | HTML 4.0 |
| `MARGINWIDTH=n` | ✓Specifies margin width for frame in pixels. | HTML 4.0 |
| `NAME="..."` | ✓Provides frame name. | HTML 4.0 |
| `NORESIZE` | ✓Prevents reader from resizing frame. | HTML 4.0 |
| `SCROLLING="..."` | ✓Specifies whether the frame can scroll in terms of `YES`, `NO`, or `AUTO`(matic). `YES` requires scrollbars; `NO` prohibits them. | HTML 4.0 |
| `SRC="URL"` | ✓Identifies source file that flows into frame. | HTML 4.0 |
| `<FRAMESET>...</FRAMESET>` | ✓Establishes frame layout. | HTML 4.0 |
| `BORDER=n` | Specifies width of border for all contained frames in pixels. | Navigator |
| `BORDERCOLOR=#rrggbb` or `"name"` | ✓Specifies color for contained frames. | IE/Navigator |
| `COLS="n, n"` | ✓Specifies column dimensions in pixels, percentage, or in terms of remaining space. `COLS="25%, 100, *"`. | HTML 4.0 |
| `FRAMEBORDER=n` | ✓Specifies border (1) or no border (0). | IE/Navigator |
| `FRAMESPACING=n` | ✓Specifies space between frames in pixels. | IE/Navigator |
| `ROWS="n, n"` | ✓Specifies row dimensions in pixels, percentage, or in terms of remaining space. `ROWS="25%, 100, *"`. | HTML 4.0 |
| `<NOFRAMES>...</NOFRAMES>` | ✓Specifies area of layout document that is visible to frame-incapable browsers. | HTML 4.0 |

cont.

*Table A-9 (continued)*

| Markup | Description | Reference or Usage |
|---|---|---|
| `<IFRAME>` | Identifies floating frame within HTML document. | HTML 4.0 |
| `ALIGN="..."` | Specifies LEFT, CENTER, RIGHT, JUSTIFY for frame alignment. | HTML 4.0 |
| `FRAMEBORDER=n` | Specifies border (1) or no border (0). | HTML 4.0 |
| `HEIGHT=n` | Specifies height for frame in pixels. | HTML 4.0 |
| `MARGINHEIGHT=n` | Specifies margin height for frame in pixels. | HTML 4.0 |
| `MARGINWIDTH=n` | Specifies margin width for frame in pixels. | HTML 4.0 |
| `NAME="..."` | Provides frame name. | HTML 4.0 |
| `SCROLLING= "..."` | Specifies whether the frame can scroll in terms of YES, NO, or AUTO(matic). Yes requires scroll bars; No prohibits them. | HTML 4.0 |
| `SRC="URL"` | Identifies source file that flows into frame. | HTML 4.0 |
| `WIDTH=n` | Specifies width of frame in pixels. | HTML 4.0 |
| `<LAYER>... </LAYER>` | Identifies layer within an HTML document. | Navigator |
| `ABOVE="..."` | Names layer that lies immediately above the current layer. | Navigator |
| `BACKGROUND= "URL"` | Specifies URL for background image for layer. | Navigator |
| `BELOW="..."` | Names layer that lies immediately beneath the current layer. | Navigator |
| `BGCOLOR= #rrggbb or "name"` | Specifies color for layer in rrggbb number or standard color name. | Navigator |
| `CLIP=x1,y1, x2,y2` | Specifies coordinates of a visible (window) rectangle in a layer. Points outside this rectangle in the layer are not visible. | Navigator |
| `LEFT=x` | Specifies the location of the frame left border in pixels from the left edge of the window. | Navigator |

| Markup | Description | Reference or Usage |
|---|---|---|
| *NAME="..."* | Provides name for layer so that it can be referenced from other frame. | Navigator |
| *SRC="URL"* | Specifies address for text to fill layer. | Navigator |
| *TOP=y* | Specifies the location of the frame top in pixels from the top of the window. | Navigator |
| *VISIBILITY= "..."* | Specifies visibility of layer in terms of SHOW, HIDE, or INHERIT (from containing layer). | Navigator |
| *WIDTH=n* | Specifies number of pixels to right border of layer at which point the text wraps. | Navigator |
| *Z-INDEX=z* | Specifies integer for stacking order. Higher numbers go on top. | Navigator |
| <MULTICOL>... </MULTICOL> | Identifies area for multiple columns. | Navigator |
| *COLS=n* | Specifies number of columns. | Navigator |
| *GUTTER=n* | Specifies width of gutter (space between columns) in pixels. | Navigator |
| *WIDTH="n"* | Specifies overall width of column area in percentage or pixels. | Navigator |

**Table A-10    Script**

| Markup | Description | Reference or Usage |
|---|---|---|
| <SCRIPT>... </SCRIPT> | ✓Marks area for script inclusion in HTML document. | HTML 4.0 |
| *LANGUAGE= "..."* | ✓Specifies scripting language, such as JavaScript or VBScript. | HTML 4.0 |
| *SRC="URL"* | ✓Specifies filename (URL) containing the script. | HTML 4.0 |
| *TYPE="..."* | ✓Specifies MIME type for script. | HTML 4.0 |

*Table A-11*   *Style Sheets (CSS1)*

| Markup | Description | Reference or Usage |
|---|---|---|
| `<SPAN>...` `</SPAN>` | ✓Marks area of document to which a specific style applies. | HTML 4.0 |
| `STYLE="..."` | ✓Defines the style for all text associated with the tag. | HTML 4.0 |
| `<STYLE>...` `</STYLE>` | ✓Indicates area within document for style definitions. | HTML 4.0 |
| `TYPE="..."` | ✓Specifies `MIME` type of style sheet. | HTML 4.0 |
| `MEDIA="..."` | ✓Specifies intended media, including screen, print, aural, all. | HTML 4.0 |

*Note:* All tags within the HTML body can accept the following attributes to apply styles.

| Markup Usage | Description | Reference or |
|---|---|---|
| `CLASS="..."` | ✓Identifies the style class associated with the tag. | HTML 4.0 |
| `ID="..."` | ✓Identifies the style ID for this one instance in the document. | HTML 4.0 |
| `STYLE="..."` | ✓Defines the style for all text associated with the tag. | HTML 4.0 |

*Table A-12*   *Object Tags*

| Markup | Description | Reference or Usage |
|---|---|---|
| `<OBJECT>...` `</OBJECT>` | Inserts an object in the page, subject to the information provided in additional tags between the opening and closing tags. | HTML 4.0 |
| `ALT="..."` | Specifies alternative text to display if the object cannot be run. | HTML 4.0 |
| `ALIGN="..."` | Places the object within the page. `RIGHT`, `MIDDLE`, and `LEFT` float the object as specified and wrap text around it. `CENTER`, `TOP`, and `BOTTOM` align relative to surrounding text. | HTML ✗ |
| `BORDER=n` | Controls the thickness of the border around object in pixels. | HTML 4.0 |

| *Markup* | *Description* | *Reference or Usage* |
|---|---|---|
| *CLASSID= "..."* | Identifies object. Precise syntax depends on object type. | HTML 4.0 |
| *CODE="..."* | Identifies the object with a standard URL, either relative or absolute. | HTML 4.0 |
| *CODEBASE="URL"* | Specifies the folder in which the object is located with a URL. Precise syntax depends on object type. | HTML 4.0 |
| *CODETYPE="URL"* | Specifies the type of object code. Precise syntax depends on object type. | HTML 4.0 |
| *DATA="URL"* | Specifies source for object data. Precise syntax depends on object type. | HTML 4.0 |
| *DECLARE* | Declares (enables) object but does not instantiate (activate) it. | HTML 4.0 |
| *HEIGHT="..."* | Specifies the height of the object in pixels. | HTML 4.0 |
| *HSPACE=n* | Specifies left and right gutter for the outside of the object in pixels. | HTML 4.0 |
| *NAME="..."* | Gives a name to the object so objects on the same page can talk with one another. | HTML 4.0 |
| *NOTAB* | Excludes object from Tab order in page. | HTML 4.0 |
| *SHAPES="..."* | Specifies shaped links in the object. | HTML 4.0 |
| *STANDBY="..."* | Identifies message to be displayed while object loads. | HTML 4.0 |
| *TABINDEX=n* | Specifies sequence number for readers who use the Tab key to maneuver around the page. | HTML 4.0 |
| *TITLE="..."* | Specifies extra information to appear with object in Internet Explorer. | HTML 4.0 |
| *TYPE="..."* | Specifies MIME type for data. | HTML 4.0 |
| *USEMAP= "mapname"* | Identifies the picture as a client-side imagemap, and specifies a MAP to use for acting on the user's clicks. | HTML 4.0 |
| *VSPACE=n* | Controls the vertical space (white space) around the object in pixels. | HTML 4.0 |

**cont.**

*Table A-12 (continued)*

| Markup | Description | Reference or Usage |
|---|---|---|
| *WIDTH=n* | Describes the object width in terms of the number of pixels or the percentage of the document width. | HTML 4.0 |
| *<PARAM ...>* | Gives parameters (other information) to an object. Place between opening and closing <OBJECT> tags. | HTML 4.0 |
| *NAME="..."* | Specifies name of parameter. Actual values depend on the object. | HTML 4.0 |
| *VALUE="..."* | Specifies value of named parameter. Actual values depend on the object. | HTML 4.0 |
| *VALUETYPE= "..."* | Specifies type of named parameter. Could be DATA, REF, OBJECT. | HTML 4.0 |

*Table A-13    Applet Tags*

| Markup | Description | Reference or Usage |
|---|---|---|
| *<APPLET>...* *</APPLET>* | ✓Inserts a Java Applet in the page, subject to the information provided in additional tags between the opening and closing tags. | HTML 3.2 ✗ |
| *ALT="..."* | ✓Specifies alternative text to display if the applet can't run. | HTML 3.2 ✗ |
| *ALIGN="..."* | ✓Places the applet LEFT, CENTER, RIGHT, TOP, MIDDLE, or BOTTOM in the page. | HTML 3.2 ✗ |
| *CODE="..."* | ✓Identifies the Java applet with a standard URL, either relative or absolute. | HTML 3.2 ✗ |
| *CODEBASE= "..."* | ✓Specifies the folder in which the applet is located with a URL. Can be omitted to default to folder in which page is located or if CODE= attribute specifies the complete URL. | HTML 3.2 ✗ |
| *HEIGHT="..."* | ✓Specifies the height of the applet in pixels. | HTML 3.2 ✗ |
| *HSPACE=n* | ✓Specifies left and right gutter for the outside of the applet in pixels. | HTML 3.2 ✗ |

| *Markup* | *Description* | *Reference or Usage* |
|---|---|---|
| *NAME="..."* | ✓Gives a name to the applet so that applets on the same page can talk with one another. | HTML 3.2 ✗ |
| *VSPACE=n* | ✓Controls the vertical space (white space) around the applet in pixels. | HTML 3.2 ✗ |
| *WIDTH="n"* | ✓Describes the applet width in terms of the number of pixels or the percentage of the document width. | HTML 3.2 ✗ |
| *TITLE="..."* | ✓Specifies extra information to appear with applet in Internet Explorer. | IE ✗ |
| <PARAM ...> | ✓Gives parameters (other information) to a Java applet. Place between opening and closing <APPLET> tags. | HTML 3.2 ✗ |
| *NAME="..."* | ✓Specifies name of parameter. Actual values depend on the applet. | HTML 3.2 ✗ |
| *VALUE="..."* | ✓Specifies value of named parameter. Actual values depend on the applet. | HTML 3.2 ✗ |

*Table A-14    Embed Tags*

| *Markup* | *Description* | *Reference or Usage* |
|---|---|---|
| <EMBED . . > | ✓Embeds an object (such as a Shockwave animation) in a Web page. | Navigator/IE ✗ |
| *HEIGHT="..."* | ✓Specifies the height of the embedded object in pixels. | Navigator/IE ✗ |
| *NAME="..."* | ✓Gives a name to the embedded object so other objects within the page can communicate with it. | Navigator/IE ✗ |
| *Other parameters* | ✓Provide other information to object as specified in the object documentation. Usually in form of WORD="value", where WORD and value are both specified in the documentation. | Navigator/IE ✗ |
| *PALETTE= #rrggbb \| #rrggbb* | ✓Specifies foreground and background colors in rrggbb colors. | Navigator/IE ✗ |

**cont.**

*Table A-14 (continued)*

| Markup | Description | Reference or Usage |
|---|---|---|
| `SRC="..."` | ✓Identifies address of information or code for the embedded object with a standard (absolute or relative) URL. | Navigator/IE ✗ |
| `UNITS="..."` | ✓Specifies units (`PIXELS` or `EN`) for the object. | Navigator/IE ✗ |
| `WIDTH=n` | ✓Specifies `WIDTH` for object `UNITS`. | Navigator/IE ✗ |
| `<PARAM ...>` | ✓Gives parameters (other information) to an applet. Place between opening and closing `<OBJECT>` tags. | Navigator/IE ✗ |
| `NAME="..."` | ✓Specifies name of parameter. Actual values depend on the applet. | Navigator/IE ✗ |
| `VALUE="..."` | ✓Specifies value of named parameter. Actual values depend on the applet. | Navigator/IE ✗ |

*Table A-15* *Internet Explorer Multimedia Extensions*

| Markup | Description | Reference or Usage |
|---|---|---|
| `<BGSOUND>` | Indicates background sounds. | IE |
| `SRC="URL"` | Indicates background sounds to play after page is opened. Sounds can be WAV, AU, or MID format. | IE |
| `LOOP="..."` | Specifies how many times (number or `"INFINITE"`) a sound plays. | IE |
| `<MARQUEE>` | Specifies a scrolling text marquee. | IE |
| `ALIGN="..."` | Specifies that the text around the marquee should align with the `TOP`, `MIDDLE`, or `BOTTOM` of the marquee. | IE |
| `BEHAVIOR="..."` | Specifies how the text should behave as `SCROLL`, `SLIDE`, or `ALTERNATE`. | IE |
| `BGCOLOR="#rrggbb"` or `"name"` | Specifies a background color for the marquee as an `rrggbb` number or standard color name. | IE |
| `DIRECTION="..."` | Specifies which direction (`LEFT` or `RIGHT`) the text should scroll. | IE |
| `HEIGHT="..."` | Specifies the height of the marquee, either in pixels or as a percentage of the screen height. | IE |

| *Markup* | *Description* | *Reference or Usage* |
|---|---|---|
| *HSPACE=n* | Specifies left and right margins for the outside of the marquee, in pixels. | IE |
| *LOOP="..."* | Specifies how many times (number or "INFINITE") a marquee will loop. | IE |
| *SCROLLAMOUNT=n* | Specifies the number of pixels between each successive progression of the marquee text. | IE |
| *SCROLLDELAY=n* | Specifies the number of milliseconds between each successive draw of the marquee text. | IE |
| *VSPACE=n* | Specifies top and bottom margins for the outside of the marquee in pixels. | IE |
| *WIDTH="n"* | Sets the width of the marquee, either in pixels or as a percentage of the screen width. | IE |

# Special Symbols

This appendix provides selected symbols that you use to include special characters in an HTML document. If you can type a specific character on your keyboard, you probably don't need to use the corresponding special symbol. If you can't type special characters, such as a letter with an umlaut, by using your keyboard, you need to use the symbols provided in this list. Tübingen, for example, becomes T&#252;bingen to come out as Tübingen in an HTML document.

According to the HTML 4.0 specification, the mnemonic name (if available) or numeric codes are equally acceptable, so all newer browsers should reproduce all these entities correctly. If you anticipate that your readers are using older browsers, however, and you make extensive use of special symbols, be sure to test your documents on as many browsers and computers as possible to make sure they appear as they should.

A number of additional symbols — mostly mathematical symbols — exist in the HTML 4.0 specification. Unfortunately, at press time, only one popular browser (Microsoft Internet Explorer) supports a significant proportion of these symbols. We've placed the whole list on our Web site at www.raycomm.com/html_reference/, so you're welcome to check out the latest and greatest symbols at your convenience. But be sure to test these symbols thoroughly before you commit to using them.

**Note:** Positions 1–31 and 127–159 in Table B-1 are not used in HTML 4.0 — we didn't just forget them. Positions 48-57 represent the numbers zero through nine, 65-90 represent capital letters, and 97-122 represent lowercase letters — we all know what they look like, so we saved a small part of a tree.

The following table shows special symbols you can use and the codes used to create them. You can type some characters and symbols in more than one way. To type the symbol Æ, for example, you can type either &#198; (from in the Numeric column) or &AElig; (from the Mnemonic column).

*Table B-1*     *Special Symbols*

| Appear As | Numeric | Mnemonic | Description |
|---|---|---|---|
|  | &#32; |  | Space |
| ! | &#33; |  | Exclamation mark |
| " | &#34; | &quot; | Quotation mark |
| # | &#35; |  | Number sign |
| $ | &#36; |  | Dollar sign |
| % | &#37; |  | Percent sign |
| & | &#38; | &amp; | Ampersand |
| ' | &#39; |  | Apostrophe |
| ( | &#40; |  | Left parenthesis |
| ) | &#41; |  | Right parenthesis |
| * | &#42; |  | Asterisk |
| + | &#43; |  | Plus sign |
| , | &#44; |  | Comma |
| - | &#45; |  | Hyphen |
| . | &#46; |  | Period (full stop) |
| / | &#47; |  | Solidus (slash) |
| : | &#58; |  | Colon |
| ; | &#59; |  | Semicolon |
| < | &#60; | &lt; | Less than |
| = | &#61; |  | Equal sign |
| > | &#62; | &gt; | Greater than |
| ? | &#63; |  | Question mark |
| @ | &#64; |  | Commercial "at" sign |
| [ | &#91; |  | Left square bracket |
| \ | &#92; |  | Reverse solidus (backslash) |
| ] | &#93; |  | Right square bracket |
| ^ | &#94; |  | Caret |
| _ | &#95; |  | Horizontal bar |
| ` | &#96; |  | Grave accent |
| { | &#123; |  | Left curly brace |
| \| | &#124; |  | Vertical bar |
| } | &#125; |  | Right curly brace |

| Appear As | Numeric | Mnemonic | Description |
|-----------|---------|----------|-------------|
| ~ | &#126; | | Tilde |
| |   |   | Nonbreaking space |
| ¡ | &#161; | &iexcl; | Inverted exclamation |
| ¢ | &#162; | &cent; | Cent sign |
| £ | &#163; | &pound; | Pound sterling |
| ¤ | &#164; | &curren; | General currency sign |
| ¥ | &#165; | &yen; | Yen sign |
| » | &#166; | &brvbar; | Broken vertical bar |
| § | &#167; | &sect; | Section sign |
| ¨ | &#168; | &uml; | Umlaut |
| © | &#169; | &copy; | Copyright |
| ª | &#170; | &ordf; | Feminine ordinal |
| ¬ | &#172; | &not; | Not sign |
| - | &#173; | &shy; | Soft hyphen |
| ® | &#174; | &reg; | Registered trademark |
| ¯ | &#175; | &macr; | Macron accent |
| ° | &#176; | &deg; | Degree sign |
| ± | &#177; | &plusmn; | Plus or minus sign |
| $^2$ | &#178; | &sup2; | Superscript two |
| $^3$ | &#179; | &sup3; | Superscript three |
| ´ | &#180; | &acute; | Acute accent |
| µ | &#181; | &micro; | Micro sign |
| ¶ | &#182; | &para; | Paragraph sign |
| · | &#183; | &middot; | Center dot |
| ¸ | &#184; | &cedil; | Cedilla |
| $^1$ | &#185; | &sup1; | Superscript one |
| º | &#186; | &ordm; | Masculine ordinal |
| » | &#187; | &raquo; | Right angle quote, guillemet right |
| ¼ | &#188; | &frac14; | Fraction one-fourth |
| ½ | &#189; | &frac12; | Fraction one-half |
| ¾ | &#190; | &frac34; | Fraction three-fourths |

cont.

*Table B-1 (continued)*

| Appear As | Numeric | Mnemonic | Description |
|---|---|---|---|
| ¿ | &#191; | &iquest; | Inverted question mark |
| À | &#192; | &Agrave; | Capital A, grave accent |
| Á | &#193; | &Aacute; | Capital A, acute accent |
| Â | &#194; | &Acirc; | Capital A, circumflex accent |
| Ã | &#195; | &Atilde; | Capital A, tilde |
| Ä | &#196; | &Auml; | Capital A, diaeresis or umlaut mark |
| Å | &#197; | &Aring; | Capital A, ring |
| Æ | &#198; | &AElig; | Capital AE diphthong (ligature) |
| Ç | &#199; | &Ccedil; | Capital C, cedilla |
| È | &#200; | &Egrave; | Capital E, grave accent |
| É | &#201; | &Eacute; | Capital E, acute accent |
| Ê | &#202; | &Ecirc; | Capital E, circumflex accent |
| Ë | &#203; | &Euml; | Capital E, diaeresis or umlaut mark |
| Ì | &#204; | &Igrave; | Capital I, grave accent |
| Í | &#205; | &Iacute; | Capital I, acute accent |
| Î | &#206; | &Icirc; | Capital I, circumflex accent |
| Ï | &#207; | &Iuml; | Capital I, diaeresis or umlaut mark |
| a | &#208; | &ETH; | Capital Eth, Icelandic |
| Ñ | &#209; | &Ntilde; | Capital N, tilde |
| Ò | &#210; | &Ograve; | Capital O, grave accent |
| Ó | &#211; | &Oacute; | Capital O, acute accent |
| Ô | &#212; | &Ocirc; | Capital O, circumflex accent |
| Õ | &#213; | &Otilde; | Capital O, tilde |
| Ö | &#214; | &Ouml; | Capital O, diaeresis or umlaut mark |
| x | &#215; | | Multiplication sign |
| Ø | &#216; | &Oslash; | Capital O, slash |
| Ù | &#217; | &Ugrave; | Capital U, grave accent |
| Ú | &#218; | &Uacute; | Capital U, acute accent |

| Appear As | Numeric | Mnemonic | Description |
|---|---|---|---|
| Û | &#219; | &Ucirc; | Capital U, circumflex accent |
| Ü | &#220; | &Uuml; | Capital U, diaeresis or umlaut mark |
| Ý | &#221; | &Yacute; | Capital Y, acute accent |
| Þ | &#222; | &THORN; | Capital THORN, Icelandic |
| ß | &#223; | &szlig; | Small sharp s, German (sz ligature) |
| à | &#224; | &agrave; | Small a, grave accent |
| á | &#225; | &aacute; | Small a, acute accent |
| â | &#226; | &acirc; | Small a, circumflex accent |
| ã | &#227; | &atilde; | Small a, tilde |
| ä | &#228; | &auml; | Small a, diaeresis or umlaut mark |
| å | &#229; | &aring; | Small a, ring |
| æ | &#230; | &aelig; | Small ae diphthong (ligature) |
| ç | &#231; | &ccedil; | Small c, cedilla |
| è | &#232; | &egrave; | Small e, grave accent |
| é | &#233; | &eacute; | Small e, acute accent |
| ê | &#234; | &ecirc; | Small e, circumflex accent |
| ë | &#235; | &euml; | Small e, diaeresis or umlaut mark |
| ì | &#236; | &igrave; | Small i, grave accent |
| í | &#237; | &iacute; | Small i, acute accent |
| î | &#238; | &icirc; | Small i, circumflex accent |
| ï | &#239; | &iuml; | Small i, diaeresis or umlaut mark |
| b | &#240; | &eth; | Small eth, Icelandic |
| ñ | &#241; | &ntilde; | Small n, tilde |
| ò | &#242; | &ograve; | Small o, grave accent |
| ó | &#243; | &oacute; | Small o, acute accent |
| ô | &#244; | &ocirc; | Small o, circumflex accent |
| õ | &#245; | &otilde; | Small o, tilde |
| ö | &#246; | &ouml; | Small o, diaeresis or umlaut mark |

cont.

*Table B-1 (continued)*

| Appear As | Numeric | Mnemonic | Description |
|---|---|---|---|
| ÷ | &#247; | | Division sign |
| ø | &#248; | &oslash; | Small o, slash |
| ù | &#249; | &ugrave; | Small u, grave accent |
| ú | &#250; | &uacute; | Small u, acute accent |
| û | &#251; | &ucirc; | Small u, circumflex accent |
| ü | &#252; | &uuml; | Small u, diaeresis or umlaut mark |
| ý | &#253; | &yacute; | Small y, acute accent |
| þ | &#254; | &thorn; | Small thorn, Icelandic |
| ÿ | &#255; | &yuml; | Small y, diaeresis or umlaut mark |

The following symbol is nonstandard. Test your intended audience before using.

| | | | |
|---|---|---|---|
| ™ | #8482; | &trade; | Trademark |

The following symbols are nonstandard, but may be useful in some cases. At press time, they worked with Netscape Navigator but not with Microsoft Internet Explorer. As always, test symbols thoroughly using several different browsers.

| Appear As | Numeric | Mnemonic | Description |
|---|---|---|---|
| — | &#8212; | &mdash; | Em dash |
| – | &#8211; | &ndash; | En dash |

Adapted from Character Entities for ISO Latin-1, © International Organization for Standardization, 1986.

# Cascading Style Sheet Reference

Appendix C provides you with a list of Cascading Style Sheets (CSS) properties and values. You find information about implementing style sheets and using them in your Web documents in Part X of this book.

You'll find much of the information provided in these tables discussed in detail in this book; some of the declarations, values, and sample rules, however, are simply provided for you to reference as your skills improve and expand. For the latest CSS reference information, see www.w3.org for the CSS specification.

Throughout this appendix, some rules apply to all elements, whereas some apply only to block-level elements. Block level HTML elements have a line break before and after (like P, H1, or BLOCKQUOTE). Inline HTML elements (like B, I, or STRONG) do not have line breaks by default.

The tables in Appendix C address the following:

- Font properties, which apply to any element containing text

- Text properties, which apply to any block level elements containing text

- Box properties, which apply margin, border, and padding formatting for all block level elements

- Color and background properties, which apply to all elements

- Classification properties, which apply formatting to lists and to control display

The tables in this appendix include three columns:

- The *Properties* column provides CSS commands. Properties with related meanings and identical possible values often appear together, separated by commas. In general, declarations work together, and various combinations of declarations can produce similar effects — there's no one right way to use these.

The meaning or effect of most properties should be fairly self-evident, particularly if you have experimented with the formatting commands in this book or in your word-processing program. When in doubt, try them out.

✔ The *Possible Values* column provides a list of each possible value (or measurement system) for the declarations. When essential, descriptions of use are also provided. Please refer to the body of the book for specific instructions. Values that are not extensively discussed in the book are likely to be fairly similar to other tags — feel free to experiment.

Some properties (shorthand properties) include all of the values from several other properties. In these cases, the Possible Values column just lists the other properties that this shorthand property can include values from.

✔ The *Sample Rule* column provides an example of the property in use. The examples should provide a starting point for use and experimentation — they're certainly not comprehensive examples of everything that style sheets can do.

Throughout this section, *length* may be measured in:

✔ percentage (%)

✔ points (pt)

✔ millimeters (mm)

✔ centimeters (cm)

✔ inches (in)

✔ picas (pc)

✔ pixels (px)

✔ x-height, which is the height of a lower-case X in the current font (ex)

✔ Em, which is the height of the capital M in the current font (em)

✔ "Normal," "none," or unspecified values from the table below take default settings. Only the differences from the normal settings must be specified.

# Cascading Style Sheets Reference

The tables in Appendix C address the following:

✔ Font Properties, which apply to any element containing text

✔ Text Properties, which apply to any block level elements containing text

- ✔ Box Properties, which apply margin, border, and padding formatting for all block level elements

- ✔ Color and Background Properties, which apply to all elements

- ✔ Classification Properties, which apply formatting to lists and to control display

## Font properties

*Note:* Font Properties can apply to any HTML element containing text (block or inline). As in HTML proper, font choices depend on the fonts available on the viewer's system.

*Table C-1*    *Font Properties*

| Property | Possible Values | Sample Rule |
|---|---|---|
| font | Shorthand property includes values from font-family, font-size, font-style, font-variant, font-weight, line-height. | P { font: Arial, sans serif bold italic } |
| font-family | Font names from reader's systems, plus generic choices of serif, sans-serif, cursive, fantasy, or monospace. Separate items with commas. | P { font-family: "Gill Sans", Arial, sans-serif } |
| font-size | xx-small, x-small, small, medium, large, x-large, xx-large, smaller, larger; percentage (%) of the previous font size; length in points (pt), millimeters (mm), centimeters (cm), inches (in), picas (pc), pixels (px), x-height (ex), or em (em) | P { font-size: large } |
| font-style | normal, italic, oblique | P { font-style: italic } |
| font-variant | normal, small-caps | P {font-variant: small-caps} |
| font-weight | normal, bold, bolder, light, lighter; values of 100, 200, 300, 400 (same as normal), 500, 600, 700 (same as bold), 800, or 900 | P {font-weight: bolder } |

## Text properties

*Note:* Text Properties can apply to any block-level HTML element containing text.

*Table C-2*    *Text Properties*

| Declaration | Possible Values | Sample Rule |
|---|---|---|
| letter-spacing | normal, length in points (pt), millimeters (mm), centimeters (cm), inches (in), picas (pc), pixels (px), x-height (ex), or em (em). | P { letter-spacing: 2px } |
| line-height | normal; multiplication factor of normal; percentage (%); length in points (pt), millimeters (mm), centimeters (cm), inches (in), picas (pc), pixels (px), x-height (ex), or em (em). | P { line-height: 200% } |
| text-align | left, right, center, justified | P { text-align: center } |
| text-decoration | none, underline, overline, line-through, blink | P {text-decoration: underline} |
| text-indent | percentage (%)of the line length; length in points (pt), millimeters (mm), centimeters (cm), inches (in), picas (pc), pixels (px), x-height (ex), or em (em) | P { text-indent: 5% } |
| text-transform | none, capitalize, uppercase, lowercase | P { text-transform: capitalize} |
| vertical-align | baseline, sub, super, top, text-top, middle, bottom, text-bottom, % (of line height) | P { vertical-align: top} |

| *Declaration* | *Possible Values* | *Sample Rule* |
|---|---|---|
| word-spacing | normal, or add length in points (pt), millimeters (mm), centimeters (cm), inches (in), picas (pc), pixels (px), x-height (ex), or em (em) | P { word-spacing: 2pt } |

## Box properties

*Note:* Box Properties can apply to any block-level HTML element, in addition to IMG, OBJECT, and similar elements. Browser support for box properties, particularly margin and border settings, is erratic. Experiment with minimal rules, then gradually expand to add the formatting you want.

*Table C-3*  *Box Properties*

| *Property* | *Possible Values* | *Sample Rule* |
|---|---|---|
| padding | Shorthand property includes values from padding-bottom, padding-left, padding-right, or padding-top. One value sets padding for all sides, two values are top and bottom, three are top, left and right, and bottom, and four specify top, right, bottom, and left in order | H2 { padding: 5% } |
| padding-bottom, padding-left, padding-right, padding-top | percentage (%); length in points (pt), millimeters (mm), centimeters (cm), inches (in), picas (pc), pixels (px), x-height (ex), orem (em) | H2 { padding-left: 10px } |
| border | Shorthand property includes values from border-width, border-style, border-color | H1 { border: thin green dotted } |
| border-bottom-width, border-left-width, border-right-width, border-top-width | thin, medium, thick; length in points (pt), millimeters (mm), centimeters (cm), inches (in), picas (pc), pixels (px), x-height (ex), or em (em) | H2 { border-left-width: thick} |

cont.

*Table C-3 (continued)*

| Property | Possible Values | Sample Rule |
|---|---|---|
| border-color | #RRGGBB number or color name | P { border-color: green } |
| border-left, border-right, border-top, border-bottom | Shorthand property includes values from border-width, border-style, or color | P { border-left: red thick solid } |
| border-style | none, dotted, dashed, solid, double, groove, ridge, inset, outset | P { border-style: dashed } |
| border-width | thin, medium, thick; length in percentage (%); or length in points (pt), millimeters (mm), centimeters (cm), inches (in), picas (pc), pixels (px), x-height (ex), or em (em) | P { border width: thick } |
| margin | Shorthand property includes values from margin-bottom, margin-left, margin-right, margin-top. One value sets margin on all sides, two values are top and bottom, three are top, left and right, and bottom, and four specify top, right, bottom, and left in order. | P { margin: 3px 6px12px } |
| margin-bottom, margin-left, margin-right, margin-top | auto; percentage (%); length in points (pt), millimeters (mm), centimeters (cm), inches (in), picas (pc), pixels (px), x-height (ex), or em (em) | P {margin-bottom: 3px } |
| clear | none, left, right, both | IMG { clear: both } |
| float | none, left, right | IMG { float: right } |
| height | auto; length in points (pt), millimeters (mm), centimeters (cm), inches (in), picas (pc), pixels (px), x-height (ex), or em (em) | H1 { height: 18px} |

| Property | Possible Values | Sample Rule |
|---|---|---|
| width | auto; length in points (pt), millimeters (mm), centimeters (cm), inches (in), picas (pc), pixels (px), x-height (ex), or em (em) | P { width: 50% } |

## Color and background properties

*Note:* Color and background properties can apply to any HTML element.

*Table C-4*    *Color and Background Properties*

| Property | Possible Values | Sample Rule |
|---|---|---|
| background | Shorthand property includes values for background-attachment, background-color, background-image, background-position, background-repeat | BODY { background: url(trees.gif) repeat-x fixed green center center } |
| background-attachment | scroll, fixed | BODY { background-attachment: fixed } |
| background-color | RRGGBB number or color name | BODY { background-color: blue } |
| background-image | url(...) | BODY { background-image: url(myphoto.jog) } |
| background position | Given in *x y* coordinates measured from upper left corner. Use %, top, center, bottom, left, center, right, length in points (pt), millimeters (mm), centimeters (cm), inches (in), picas (pc), pixels (px), x-height (ex) or em (em) | BODY { background-position: top center} |
| background-repeat | repeat, repeat-x, repeat-y, no-repeat | BODY { background-repeat: repeat-x } |
| color | RRGGBB number or color name | P { color: 339966 } |

## Classification properties

*Note:* Classification properties can apply to most HTML elements. In addition to controlling list formatting and text wrap, classification properties can change HTML elements from block to in-line or back.

*Table C-5*     *Classification Properties*

| Property | Possible Values | Sample Rule |
|---|---|---|
| display | none, block, in-line, list-item | PRE { display: none } |
| list-style, list-style-type | disc, circle, square, decimal, lower-roman, upper-roman, lower-alpha, upper-alpha, none | LI { list-style: lower-alpha } |
| list-style-image | url(...) | LI { list-style-image: url(bullet.gif) |
| list-style-position | inside, outside | LI { list-style-position: outside } |
| white-space | normal, pre, nowrap | H1 { white-space: nowrap } |

# *Index*

## Symbols

! tag, 119, 161
!DOCTYPE tag, 21
#INCLUDE attribute, 119

## A

A tag, 41
absolute URLs, 36, 38
acute accents, 205
ACTION attribute, 124
ADDRESS tag, 95
addresses. *See also* URLs
    obtaining for Web pages, 117
    Web pages, adding to, 95
Adobe Photoshop, 51
ALIGN attribute, 60, 91, 108, 142
alignment
    effects and, 64
    images, 60–63, 172, 173
    multiple options, 63
    text, 108, 110
    text, default, 108
ALINK attribute, 106
ALT attribute, 48
ALT tag, 50
alternative content, 149
alternative text (ALT tag), 50
ampersands, 204
anchor tags, 36, 40
    HREF attribute, 40
    NAME attribute, 41
anchors
    images as, 68
    internal targets, 45
    name anchors, 45
angle brackets (<>), 19
angle quotation marks, 205
apostrophes, 204
applets, embedded, 175, 198, 199
applications
    ftp, 118
    server programs, 118
AREA tag, 81
asterisks, 204
at signs, 204

attributes, 18
    anchor tags, 40, 41
    FORM tag, 124
    forms, 124
    input fields, 126
    lists, 33
    server-side includes, 119
    tables, 88
    values for forms, 124
author contact information, 94, 96
automatic linking, 119, 120

## B

B tag, 28, 29
BACKGROUND attribute, 102
background images, 55, 102, 104, 171, 172
    GIF files, 56
    locating, 104
    seamless, 105
    tiling, 104
backgrounds
    color, 170
    color, applying, 100, 101
    color, selecting, 102
    selecting, 105
    testing, 105
    troubleshooting, 104
    URLs, 103
    vertical bands, 105
backslashes, 204
banner document, 147
BGCOLOR attribute, 100
BLOCKQUOTE tag, 33
BODY tag, 21, 23
bold text, 29
border attribute, 90, 150, 152
BORDERCOLOR attribute, 150
borders, 48
    frames, 151, 153
    images, 72
    increasing thickness, 90
    table cells, adding to, 90
    tables, 90
box properties, cascading style sheets, 213
BR tag, 93
breaks, lines, 93

**broken vertical bars, 205**
**browsers**
  closing table tags, 88
  compatibility, 142
  style sheet support, 158
  Web pages, appearance differences, 4
**BUTTON tag, 128**
**buttons, adding to forms, 127, 128**

# C

**carets, 204**
**cascading style sheets, 162, 210**
  box properties, 213
  classification properties, 216
  color properties, 215
  font properties, 211
  text properties, 212
**case sensitivity, 19**
  URLs, 37
**cedillas, 205**
**cells**
  borders, adding, 90
  tables, 89
**cent signs, 205**
**cgi-bin directory, server programs and, 118**
**character-level tags, 175, 181, 183**
**check boxes**
  creating, 129–131
  forms, adding to, 128, 130, 132, 133
**CHECKED attribute, 127**
  troubleshooting, 134
**circular imagemaps, 77, 79**
**circumflex accents, 206**
**classification properties, cascading style sheets, 216**
**clear all attribute, 94**
**clickable areas, mapping, 76**
**clickable images.** *See* imagemaps
**client-side imagemaps, 74**
**clip art, 54**
**closing tags, 18**
**colons, 204**
**color**
  background, 170
  backgrounds, applying to, 100, 101
  depth, file size and, 58
  dithering, images, 52
  hexadecimal numbering system, 53
  images, 52
  links, setting, 107, 108
  RGB (Red Green Blue), 52
  RGB values, 101
  RGB values, selecting, 102
  selecting by name, 101
  selecting by RGB value, 101
  text, 170
  text, setting, 105, 107, 108
**COLOR attribute, 111**
**COLS attribute, 150**
**column tags, 175, 185, 190**
**commands, deprecated, 158**
**commas, 204**
**components, adding to forms, 126–144**
**compression, image files, 58**
**contact information, 94, 96**
**content development, 148, 149**
  alternative content, 149
**coordinates, imagemaps, 77**
  circles, 79
  polygons, 80
  rectangles, 78
**COORDS attribute, 81, 83**
**copyright signs, 205**
**copyrights, images and, 54**
**counters, 118**
  Web pages, including in, 120, 121
**curly braces ({ }), style rules, 165**

# D

**DATE LOCAL attribute, 119**
**degree signs, 205**
**deprecated commands, 158**
**developing content, 148, 149**
**diaeresis, 206**
**directories**
  cgi-bin, 118
  Internet, 23
**directory name (URLs), 37, 38**
**documents**
  body, 23
  fonts, 168, 169
  frameset documents, 149, 150, 151, 152
  images, inserting, 49
  linking, 36
  linking within site, 41, 42
  links in, 44
  links to other sites, 42, 43
  paragraphs, 27
  style sheets, connecting, 160, 161, 162, 163, 164
  title, 22
**dollar signs, 204**
**dots, 205**
**downloading images, speed, 57, 58**

drawings. *See* images
drop-down lists. *See* select lists

## E

e-mail
   forms, receiving results, 124
   links, including in Web pages, 96
ECHO VAR attribute, 119
em dashes, 208
EM tag, 28
embedded applet tags, 175, 198, 199
embedded object tags, 175, 197
embedding style sheets, 161
embedding tags, 200
emphasizing text, 28
en dashes, 208
equal signs, 204
exclamation marks, 204
extensions for server-side includes, 119

## F

FACE attribute, 111
feminine ordinal signs, 205
Fetch, 118
FIELDSET tag, 141, 143
FILE attribute, 119
file extensions for server-side includes, 119
file name (URLs), 37
files
   images, size, 58
   photographs, 58
   style sheets, 163
font properties, cascading style sheets
   and, 211
FONT tag, 111
fonts
   document-wide, 168, 169
   style sheets, 166
FORM tag, 124
form tags, 175, 193
formats, images, 51
formatting
   document wide, 160
   style sheets, 158
   text, 19
forms
   attribute values, 124
   check boxes, adding, 128, 130, 132, 133
   components, adding, 126–144

   creating, 125, 126
   hidden input areas, adding, 136
   input fields, adding, 126, 128
   password input areas, adding, 136
   radio buttons, adding, 128, 130, 132, 133
   receiving results, 124
   sections, grouping, 141, 143
   select lists, adding, 136, 138
   Submit and Reset buttons, adding, 127, 128
   text areas, adding, 139, 141
   text input areas, adding, 134, 135
   troubleshooting, 134
   uses, 124
fractions, 205
FRAME tag, 152
frame tags, 175, 193, 196
FRAMEBORDER attribute, 150, 152
frames, 145, 146
   borders, 151, 153
   disadvantages, 147
   resizing, 154
   scrolling, 154
   setup, 152, 153, 154
   testing, 155
frameset documents, 149, 150, 151, 152
FRAMESET tag, 150, 153
FTP (File Transfer Protocol) sites, 118
   linking to, 44
FTP Explorer, 118

## G

general currency signs, 205
German sharp s, 207
GIF files, 48
   background images, 56
GraphicConverter for Macintosh, images
   and, 52
graphics. *See also* images
grave accents, 204
greater than signs, 204

## H

H1 tag, 25
H2 tag, 25
H3 tag, 25
H4 tag, 25
H5 tag, 25
H6 tag, 25
HEAD tag, 21, 22, 161

headings, 25
   tables, creating in, 89
HEIGHT attribute, 59
hexadecimal numbers, 53
   RGB values, 101
hidden input areas, forms, 136
hit counters, 118
   Web pages, including in, 120, 121
horizontal bars, 204
horizontal rules, 91, 93
   applying, 91, 92
   cautions, 93
   style sheets, 91
horizontal spacing, 65
host name (URLs), 37
hot spots, 36. *See also* links
HR tag, 91, 93
HREF attribute, 40, 41, 81, 163
HSPACE attribute, 61
HTML 4 For Dummies, 161
HTML Body Markup tags, 175, 179, 180
HTML documents, linking style sheets, 163, 164
HTML pages. *See also* Web pages
   changes, automating, 120
   changing, 117
   code-based editors, 7
   creating, 8
   HTML code appearance, 2
   opening, 9
   placing on servers, 116, 118
   publishing, 6, 7, 11, 116
   saving, 9, 10
   testing, 5
   text editors, 6
   Web page appearance, 4
   WYSIWYG editors, 7
HTML servers. *See* servers
HTML Structural Markup tags, 175, 177, 179
HTML tag, 21, 22
http (protocol indicator), 37
http servers. *See* servers
hyperlinks. *See* links
hypertext anchors, 175, 183, 184
hyphens, 204

**I**

I tag, 28, 29
Icelandic capital Eth, 206
Icelandic capital THORN, 207
Icelandic small Eth, 207
Icelandic small thorn, 208

image tags, 175, 184, 185
imagemaps, 74
   circles, 79
   circular, 77
   client-side, 74
   coordinates, 77
   defining, 81
   images, adding, 75
   mapping clickable areas, 76
   polygons, 77, 80
   rectangles, 78
   rectangular, 77
   server-side, 74
images, 48. *See also* graphics
   alignment, 60, 61, 62, 63, 172, 173
   ALT tag, 50
   anchors, 68
   background, 55, 102, 104, 171, 172
   background, locating, 104
   background, seamless, 105
   borders, 48, 72
   borrowing from other Web sites, 54
   clip art, 54
   color, 52
   copyright issues, 54
   creating, 51, 52
   dimensions, 59
   dithering (color), 52
   documents, inserting in, 49
   download speed, 57, 58
   file compression, 58
   file size, 58
   formats, 51
   freeware software, 56
   GIF files, 48
   GraphicConverter for Macintosh, 52
   hexadecimal numbering system, color and, 53
   JPG files, 48
   links, 68
   PaintShop Pro for Windows, 52
   photographs, 58
   PNG files, 48
   shareware software, 56
   size, 59
   style sheets, 60
   thumbnails, 70
   thumbnails, links, 71
   TIF files, 52
   tiling, 104
   transparent, 55
   white space, 61
   xv for UNIX, 52
IMG SRC tag, 48, 75

**IMG tag, 59**
**inheritance, 160**
**input areas**
   hidden, adding to forms, 136
   passwords, adding to forms, 136
   text, adding to forms, 134, 135
**input fields, forms, 126, 128**
**INPUT tag, 126**
**internal links, 44**
**internal targets, 45**
**Internet directories, 23**
**Internet Explorer Multimedia Extensions tags, 175, 200, 201**
**Internet Service Providers.** *See* ISPs
**intranets, 116**
   creating, 16
**inverted exclamation marks, 205**
**inverted question marks, 206**
**ISMAP attribute, 75**
**ISPs (Internet Service Providers)**
   URLs for personal Web pages, 117
**italic text, 29**

**J**

JPG files, 48

**L**

**LAST MODIFIED attribute, 119**
**layer tags, 175, 193, 196**
**LEDGEND tag, 141, 143**
**left curly braces, 204**
**left parenthesis, 204**
**left square brackets, 204**
**less than signs, 204**
**LI tag, 30**
**ligatures, 206**
**line breaks, 93**
**LINK attribute, 106**
**LINK tag, 163**
**linking style sheets, 162, 163**
**linking tags, 175, 183, 184**
**links**
   anchor tags, 36
   automatic, 119, 120
   color, setting, 107, 108
   documents, 44
   documents in other sites, 42, 43
   documents within site, 41, 42
   FTP sites, 44
   imagemaps, 74

   images, 68
   images, borders, 72
   internal, 44
   mailto, 96
   overview, 36
   server-side includes, 119
   setup, 154, 155
   URLs, 36
**list tags, 175, 181**
**lists, 30, 31**
   attributes, 33
   numbered lists, 30
   ordered, 32
   ordered lists, 30

**M**

**macron accents, 205**
**mailto link, 96**
**MAP tag, 81**
**mapping clickable areas, 76**
**markup tags, 19**
**masculine ordinals, 205**
**MAXLENGTH attribute, 127**
**META tag, 23**
**METHOD attribute, 124**
**micro signs, 205**
**Microsoft Web Publishing Wizard, 118**
**MULTIPLE attribute, 136, 139**
**multiplication signs, 206**

**N**

**name anchors, 45**
**NAME attribute, 41, 81, 127, 137, 152**
**names**
   frames, 147
   servers, 116
**naming conventions, 38**
**navigation document, 147**
**nesting tags, 19**
**newsletters, 14**
**NOFRAMES attribute, 150**
**NOFRAMES tags, 151**
**NOHREF attribute, 82**
**nonbreaking spaces, 205**
**NORESIZE attribute, 152**
**not signs, 205**
**number symbols, 204**
**numbered lists, 30**

## O

objects, embedded tags for, 175, 197
OL tag, 30, 32
opening tags, 18
OPTION attribute, 137
ordered lists, 30, 32
organization names, URLs, 117

## P

P tag, 27, 32
Paint Shop Pro for Windows, images and, 52
pairs, tags. *See* tags
paragraph signs, 205
paragraphs, 27
parentheses, 204
password input areas, forms, 136
percent signs, 204
periods, 204
personal Web pages, 13, 14
photographs, file formats, 58
Photoshop (Adobe), 51
pictures. *See* images
plus signs, 204
plus/minus sign, 205
PNG files, 48
polygon imagemaps, 77, 80
port numbers, URLs, 38
pound sterling signs, 205
precedence, inheritance, 160
protocol indicator (URLs), 37
publishing HTML pages, 6, 11, 116

## Q

question marks, 204
quotation marks, 204
quoted text, 33

## R

radio buttons
    creating, 132, 133
    forms, 128, 130, 132, 133
rectangular imagemaps, 77, 78
registered trademark signs, 205
REL attribute, 163
relative URLs, 36, 39
reset button, 128

Reset buttons, 127
RGB, values, 101, 102
RGB color (Red Green Blue), 52
right curly braces, 204
right parenthesis, 204
right square brackets, 204
ring marks, 206
ROWS attribute, 150
rows in tables, 89

## S

script tags, 175, 196
SCROLLING attribute, 152
scrolling in frames, 154
seamless background images, 105
search programs, 116
search services, 23
section signs, 205
security, server programs and, 118
select lists
    expanding, 138
    forms, adding to, 136, 138
    multiple selections, 139
SELECT tag, 136
SELECTED attribute, 137
semicolons, 204
server programs, counters, 120, 121
server-side imagemaps, 74
server-side includes, 119
servers, 116
    directories for HTML pages, 116
    HTML pages, placing on, 118
    intranets, 116
    names, 116
    security, 118
    server programs, 118
    types of PCs, 116
SHAPE attribute, 82
sharp s, 207
size
    frames, 154
    images, 59
size attribute, 91, 111, 127, 137
slash (/), 18, 204
    closing tags, 18
    URLs and, 39
slashed capital Os, 206
soft hyphens, 205
spaces, 204

**spacing**
horizontal, 65
table headings, adding to, 89
vertical, 65
**SRC attribute, 152**
**STRONG tag, 28**
**structure tags, 20**
!DOCTYPE, 21
BODY, 23
HEAD, 22
HTML, 22
META, 23
TITLE, 22
**style sheet tags, 175, 196**
**style sheets, 157**
background color, 100
background images, 171, 172
backgrounds, tiling, 105
browser support, 158
cascading, 210, 214, 216
cascading style sheets, 162
color, background, 170
color, text, 170
constructing rules, 165, 166
documents, connecting to, 160–164
embedding, 161
files, 163
fonts, 166, 168, 169
horizontal rules, 91
HTML documents, linking to, 163, 164
image alignment, 60, 172, 173
linking, 162, 163
overview, 158
type specifications, 110, 112, 113
**STYLE tag, 161**
**Submit buttons, 127, 128**
**superscripts, 205**

**T**

**table tags, 175, 185, 190**
**tables**
attributes, 88
borders, 90
borders, adding to cells, 90
borders, increasing thickness, 90
cells, 89
closing tags, 88
creating, 88, 90
headings, creating, 89
rows, creating, 89
tags, 88

troubleshooting, 90
uses, 88
**tags, 18.** *See also* **individual tag names**
anchor tags, 36, 40
character-level, 175, 181, 183
closing, 88
closing tags, 18
columns, 175, 185, 190
embedded applets, 175, 198, 199
embedded objects, 175, 197
embedding, 200
forms, 124, 175, 193
frames, 175, 193, 196
headings, 25
HTML Body Markup, 175, 179, 180
HTML Structural Markup, 175, 177, 179
hypertext anchors, 175, 183, 184
images, 175, 184, 185
Internet Explorer Multimedia Extensions, 175, 200, 201
layers, 175, 193, 196
links, 175, 183, 184
lists, 175, 181
markup, 19
nesting, 19
opening tags, 18
pairs, 18
scripts, 175, 196
server-side includes, 119
structure tags, 20
style sheets, 175, 196
tables, 88, 175, 185, 190
text, 111
**TARGET attribute, 154**
**targets**
internal, 45
setup, 154, 155
**TD tag, 88**
**testing**
backgrounds, 105
frames, 155
HTML pages, 5
**text, 18**
aligning, 108, 110
aligning, default, 108
background color, selecting, 101
bold, 29
color, 170
color, setting, 105, 107, 108
emphasizing, 28
formatting, 19
italic, 29

quoted, 33
type specifications, 110, 112, 113
**text areas, forms, 139, 141**
**TEXT attribute, 106**
**text editors, 6**
WYSIWYG editors, 7
**text input areas, forms, 134, 135**
**text properties, cascading style sheets, 212**
**TH tag, 88**
**thumbnails (images), 70**
linking to larger images, 71
**TIF files, 52**
**tildes, 205**
**tiling images, 104**
**TITLE tag, 21, 22**
**TR tag, 88**
**trademarks, 208**
**transparent images, 55**
GIF files, 56
**troubleshooting**
backgrounds, 104
CHECKED attribute, 134
tables, 90
**TYPE attribute, 127, 161, 163**
**type specifications, 110, 112, 113**

**U**

**UL tag, 30, 31**
**umlauts, 205, 206**
**URLs (Uniform Resource Locators).** *See also*
**addresses**
absolute, 36, 38
background images, 103
basic names, 116
case sensitivity, 37
definition of, 36
directory name, 37, 38
file name, 37
host name, 37
links and, 36
obtaining, 117
organization names, obtaining, 117
port numbers, 38
protocol indicator, 37
relative, 36, 39
slash (/) and, 39
virtual names, 117
**USEMAP attribute, 75**

**V**

**VALUE attribute, 127, 128, 137**
**vertical bands (backgrounds), 105**
**vertical bars, 204**
**vertical spacing, 65**
**VIRTUAL attribute, 119**
**virtual domains, 117**
**VLINK attribute, 106**
**VSPACE attribute, 61**

**W**

**Web pages.** *See also* **HTML pages**
changes, automating, 120
changing, 117
creating, 8
newsletters, creating, 14
opening, 9
personal, creating, 13, 14
placing on servers, 116, 118
publishing, 11, 116
saving, 9, 10
search programs, 116
**Web Publishing Wizard (Microsoft), 118**
**Web servers.** *See* **servers**
**Web sites, 36**
images, borrowing, 54
linking documents within, 41, 42
linking to, 42, 43
**Web-authoring applications, 118**
**white space, images and, 61**
**WIDTH attribute, 59, 91**
**WS-FTP, 118**
**WYSIWYG editors, 7**

**X**

**xv for UNIX, images and, 52**

**Y**

**yen signs, 205**

# Notes

# Notes

# IDG BOOKS WORLDWIDE BOOK REGISTRATION

Register This Book and Win!

## We want to hear from you!

Visit **http://my2cents.dummies.com** to register this book and tell us how you liked it!

- ✔ Get entered in our monthly prize giveaway.

- ✔ Give us feedback about this book — tell us what you like best, what you like least, or maybe what you'd like to ask the author and us to change!

- ✔ Let us know any other *For Dummies®* topics that interest you.

Your feedback helps us determine what books to publish, tells us what coverage to add as we revise our books, and lets us know whether we're meeting your needs as a *For Dummies* reader. You're our most valuable resource, and what you have to say is important to us!

Not on the Web yet? It's easy to get started with *Dummies 101®: The Internet For Windows® 98* or *The Internet For Dummies®3* at local retailers everywhere.

Or let us know what you think by sending us a letter at the following address:

*For Dummies* Book Registration
Dummies Press
10475 Crosspoint Blvd.
Indianapolis, IN 46256

**BESTSELLING BOOK SERIES**